THAT THEY MAY BE ONE

THAT THEY MAY BE ONE

Cedric C. Adams

To order additional copies of this book, contact:
Xlibris Corporation
1-888-795-4274
www.Xlibris.com
Orders@Xlibris.com
63047

CONTENTS

This book is dedicated to the primary covenant community in my life—
my queen and eternal wife Tonya, my sons LaDarrius (the king) and
D'Anthony (the rock), and my baby-girl Chelsea, who is not with our
covenant community physically any longer but always in Daddy's heart,
and to our God-children.

ACKNOWLEDGEMENTS

Thank you to my family for your patient willingness to sacrifice special moments so that I could get this work done for the global covenant community, The Kingdom of God.

Thank you to the first covenant community that I have had the privilege of overseeing, Hope of Glory. You all are the best people in the world in my eyes. Your prayers and support have meant so much to your spiritual father.

Thank you to Divine Covenant Assembly and Covenant Connection. Your true spirit of covenant can never be denied. You have embraced me with so much love and appreciation for what God has given me. I am thankful to be a part of such a powerful, synergistic association of ministry gifts.

Thank you to my Presbyters who have prayed me through this process and lent me your ears—Mother Glorice Adams (Granny), Pastor Alvin Pope, Apostle Michael Stevenson, Superintendent Robert Sample, and Apostle Lawrence Windom.

Lastly, thank you to all who have supported me through the years in love, prayer, prophecy, finance, assistance, and opening your doors to the ministry that God has graced unto me.

INTRODUCTION

"One band, one sound" is the popular motto of Doctor Lee from one of the hit movies amongst today's African American young adults, "Drum Line." This philosophy, perpetuated by the good doctor, was intended to bring all of the members of the band to recognize that there was no room for individual showboating that would undermine the overall objective of the band. Dr. Lee, played by Orlando Jones, had his work cut out for him when he brought an egocentric, talented young man named Devon, played by the multitalented actor Nick Canon, who did not share his philosophy initially. As a matter of fact, this young man proved to corrupt others from the simplicity of Dr. Lee's philosophical approach to music. In the end, Dr. Lee will demonstrate that the motto of this marching band is beyond a doubt the declaration of musical greatness.

Dr. Lee's musical philosophy, when perceived beyond the obvious, speaks the sentiments of the heart of the resurrected Savior who prior to His death prayed to the Father, "that they may be one even as you and I are one." This request of Christ was released four times in the seventeenth chapter of John, which suggests that this cry was not just a fundamental desire but emphatically it was the longing of the heart of Christ. While many find it important to compete for rank and clout, the longing of Jesus is clear, "that they may be one". In this moment of passion, Jesus brings all Kingdom citizens, ambassadors and sons to a place of common ground in God.

A parade of titles, clothes, greed, and manipulation is typical of the common church of today. Euclid, the Greek mathematician said, "the whole is greater than the sum of its parts." Oh that the body of Christ would come to this understanding. The present state of the church is one of competition, rebellion, and rejection. This was not the aspiration of the manufacturer of the church, rather, His longing was for the church to operate as a unit of driven soldiers who are compelled through their common love for Christ and for one another. In the

21st century, the church cannot continue its course of highly visible competitions of performance. As the dry bones of Ezekiel's valley, we must come together bone to bone and supply strength to one another until we fulfill the prophecy to live as an exceedingly great army.

Many in the church world have succumbed to the artificial blockades of community, known as individualism and humanism, which only lead to a perpetuation of division and isolation. Thankfully, there are some who have already embraced community and others who will hear the passionate cry of Christ to manifest a common unity.

Some churches have even attempted to eradicate the obvious division and separation of the saints in the local church and beyond through pseudo displays of love as the saints parade around the room and hug one another after being prompted by a minister. While at first glance this appears to be a true moment of intimacy (which it should be) among the saints, the indictment is that many times we only touch or even worse only speak to one another when we are prompted to do so.

Is it possible that the church that Jesus died for could come to a place of true unity to fulfill purpose and release an unquenchable destiny in the earth? I say, not only is it possible, but out of the church shall come a people who will disregard the popular opinion of the masses seeking to promote their own agenda. This remnant will cause massive deliverance and fortified wholeness to be released in the earth, the likes of which we have never known experientially.

If you are one who is very concerned about being a part of a covenant community and not just a church member, begin to seek the Lord for deliverance from the hurts of the past. Perhaps the church that you are in now is or is becoming a covenant community. If so, submit to that fellowship of believers wholeheartedly and be involved in the community. If not, seek God for direction as to the place where you are to be planted so that you may be actively engaged and involved with the community. Yes, there is a degree of vulnerability to covenant community, but remember, covenant community is God's idea and we must be willing to submit to God. He knows your hurts from the past and he knows exactly where to place you where you may receive total healing and restoration. People have all types of reasons for joining a local church or a fellowship of churches. WARNING—do not attend because your family and/or friends are in attendance or because there is a long list of monetary benefits that seem to be available to you. Join because you feel the tug of the Spirit agreeing that within the house is a community of believers that will edify and strengthen you to accomplish all that God has ordained for your life.

The movie, "Barbershop", has helped to foster my understanding of covenant community along with "Drumline". Calvin, played by Ice Cube, inherits his father's neighborhood barbershop only to sell it because of his personal ambitions. Eddie, played by Cedric the Entertainer, displays tremendous disgust with this action taken by Calvin. For those who are not familiar with the African American community, the barbershop is a community within the community. Calvin puts the community in jeopardy to pursue his own agenda. This community is so important to some people that they spend the entire day at the barbershop like Checker Fred while others drop in to collect funds for a young man to purchase shoes for his college endeavors. The barbershop is the place where people are allowed to speak their opinions no matter how controversial, because when the dust clears it is understood that the barbershop is a place for all people to come together in unity. If this is true for a neighborhood barbershop, how much more should this be true of the church, local and universal?

I would like for us to look at one more portrayal of community based on Jesus' instructions to his disciples to consider the birds of the air. Have you ever noticed that a flock of geese almost always flies together in a formation? As each bird flaps its wings, it creates uplift for the bird following. By flying in a V formation, the flock's flying range is 71% greater than if each bird flew alone. Whenever a goose falls out of the formation, it suddenly feels the drag and resistance of trying to fly alone and quickly gets back in formation to take advantage of the "lifting power" of the bird immediately in front. When a goose gets sick, wounded, or shot down, two geese drop out of formation and follow it down to protect it. It seems that Jesus said to consider the birds because they understand the Bible. Ecclesiastes 4:9-12, The Living Bible, "Two can accomplish more than twice as much as one, for the results can be much better. If one falls, the other pulls him up; but if a man falls when he is alone, he's in trouble. Also, on a cold night, two under the same blanket gain warmth from each other, but how can one be warm alone? And one standing alone can be attacked and defeated, but two can stand back-to-back and conquer; three is even better, for a triple-braided cord is not easily broken."

Whether you are one of the saints or the leader of a house, this book will challenge you to find strength and comfort in the arms of a true covenant community that will manifest Christ in the earth. I believe with all of my heart that covenant community is the key to the ultimate fulfillment of the true church thus releasing the manifestation of the Kingdom of God in the earth. Let's explore this mandate together and go where many will choose not to go and be left behind with handfuls of purpose, while the rest of us take on the true nature of the King.

The nature of the King released through men has been the plan of God since the inception of this new kind of species that all of eternity and creation had never seen before. God speaks the language of community from the beginning of man's existence. "Let us make man in our image and after our likeness" is the declaration of the King. Therefore, it is not heretical for me to pronounce that the common union that we share in as men extends beyond our harmony with one another in the flesh. Mankind is to function in the earth as God's duplication species.

The challenge arises when man steps out of sync with the order of God. This unfortunately leads us to the excommunication of Adam from the garden. Notice, verse 24 of Genesis 3 says that God drove the man out of the garden—not drove THEM but rather drove the MAN. It seems like someone is missing from the text. Why does the scripture not say that God drove them out of the garden? God speaks the same language at the end of chapter three that he spoke in Genesis 1:26. He refers to man to speak of the community. Perhaps, this is the same method taken by the Apostle Paul in Ephesians 4:13 . . ." till we all come to the unity of the faith and of the knowledge of the Son of God, *to a perfect man*, to the measure of the stature of the fullness of Christ" (New King James Version). We must become a man, a corporate man, a Covenant Community.

This coming together in unity is not one that is birthed in the flesh. True covenant community is birth in the spirit to release the divine nature among us. What the first man Adam lost, the last man Adam restored. We are to walk in complete harmony with God as His duplicates in the earth realm. The time has come for the manifestation of the sons of God. We do not have time to just build mausoleums unto ourselves. Let's become Mount Zion, by any means necessary, even if it means swallowing pride and repenting from dead church works.

As we approach this broad topic of recapturing the glory of oneness, we will begin by looking at the local covenant community. In the fourth chapter of Ephesians, the Apostle Paul speaks of the ascension gift ministries within the Body of Christ. These ministry gifts are empowered and released on local, regional, and international levels. On that premise, we will explore covenant community beyond the local setting and move into the regional and international applications. The ultimate assignment of the ascension gift ministries is to bring about the restoration of all things to the original intent of the Father. They must bring us beyond oneness with man into the glory of oneness with God.

CHAPTER 1

No More "Church" as Usual

Imagine a typical Sunday in the life of a Christian family. The Johnson's awaken early on Sunday morning to dress in their finest clothes. This is the day that their children are allowed to wear their "church shoes." Though they search high and low for pantyhose, "church socks," and the perfect tie, they never have to search for their Bibles. The Bibles are exactly where they were placed a week ago. Anne, the mother, picks up her Bible, and they are off to The First Church of The Last Day. As they enter church, a squad of men is seated together at the front of the church. One man kneels down beside his chair to recite a prayer that everyone knows by heart while the other men moan and groan and bellow, "Yes, Father God." As the deacons are praying, a "mother" in the church is allowed to start the first lines of a hymn and the congregation immediately joins in. Shortly thereafter, under the watchful eyes of the deacon board sitting on the front row, the Reverend Doctor mounts the pulpit to preach his sermon, careful not to touch any subjects that might be too sensitive for the deacons who seemingly are nodding in agreement; yet the truth is that they are passing to and from consciousness and unconsciousness. Children squirm restlessly on the pews while mothers use pinches to make them sit still and listen until they slowly but surely wander off into dreamland. No one seems to notice the members of the choir passing notes and cracking jokes all through the message. All of this drama is going on until of course the preacher says, "Say amen" or "Say yes". Suddenly, after 30 minutes of rhetoric, the musician notes it's time to find the key of F so the preacher can get ready to close. Suddenly, the entire service is in an uproar and some sleepy deacon awakens and says, "You preaching now preacha" as the preacher confirms that now he feels his help coming. After 7 minutes of hooping, the offering plate is passed down each aisle and adults drop in a few one-dollar bills while the few children not asleep drop in loose change. After the benediction, the church members hug and converse (except for the ones who don't like each other), affirming their agreement that "service sure was good." A few of them discuss upcoming programs like the annual choir day or "The 100 Women in White Day." As the Johnson's return home, they cease their thoughts about God and church as easily as they change out of their Sunday garb and transition into "around the house clothes." They will repeat the exact same routine next week . . . but for now, church is over.

Episodes like this one take place in almost every city and town in our country as untaught Christians think they are fulfilling their Christian duty. Appearances would indicate that these families are *doing* what they should be doing, yet I would say that they are not *being* who they should be. Herein lies the breakdown of the traditional church; believers are *doing* church when they should be *being* the church. The picture painted above is of a deacon-dominated church often ruled according to a masculine agenda where women are not respected as ministers to and for God. No one dares to "rock the boat" with an idea that could be considered radical. Children are expected to digest the sermons preached to an adult congregation and leaders are afraid to teach the members anything revelatory that challenges their traditions. Programs proceed as planned; no space is permitted for the unpredictable. The church "service" ends with most attendees not realizing that the service of ministry should begin as they leave the church parking lot. Sadly, many continue with their lives touched but unchanged, impressed but not impacted.

Many members of traditional churches are disillusioned at the church's lifelessness and stagnancy. Potential members are deterred by religious politics and church cliques. Both groups suffer by living defeated lives at the hands of church leaders who insist, "We've always done it this way," and "If it ain't broke, don't fix it." The truth is not only is it broken but ineffectual and in dreadful need of repair. What we have come to know as church must be transformed from a religious obligation to a progressive movement. This progressive movement will be the result of a revolutionary revelation that will lead to a great paradigm shift.

First used by scientist Thomas Kuhn in 1962, "a paradigm shift can be thought of as a change from one way of thinking to another. It's a revolution, a transformation, a sort of metamorphosis. It just does not happen, but rather it is driven by agents of change" (www.taketheleap.com).

The term "paradigm shift" can be applied to any area of expertise: business, science, technology, or fashion. Leaders, whose ears are open to hear the voice of the Lord, whose eyes are focused on the kingdom of God, and whose hearts are in sync with the heartbeat of God, are undoubtedly aware of the great paradigm shift within the church. Unfortunately, many remain blind, deaf, and insensitive to the move of God. The result of this ignorance is the traditional church mindset, oblivious to the shifting that's taking place in the Spirit.

Opponents to change often, unjustly, quote the scripture according to Hebrews 13:8, "Jesus Christ is the same yesterday, today, and forever." While it is true that his nature and essence does not change, God's methods for dealing with his people are constantly changing. For instance, we do not have to bring heifers and goats when we go to our respective temples of worship. This is the result of God's method changing. Let's look at the life of Abraham, who was told to offer his son as a sacrifice by God and then told not to do so. He was instead instructed to use the ram in the bush by the same God. The principle here is the proceeding word of God. We will never fulfill the mandate to strategically proceed without hearing the proceeding word of God.

Each generation is supposed to come to new places in God that generations previously did not move into. This is what I have termed Generational Progression. For example, Moses will lead the children of Israel to the Red Sea and then stop to get instructions from God. God will tell Moses to stretch out his rod and the water will depart so that the children of Israel would walk across on dry ground. By the time the Joshua generation would come to a body of water, the Jordan River, he will get different instructions from the same God. He will have to let the priests bearing the ark get their feet in the water first and then the water would depart. If this were the end of God's method changing that would be enough to prove my point. Yet we have one more instance of a generation taking a journey and having to contend with a body of water. Jesus himself will come to a large body of water and he will need no rod, nor will he need the water to part. He just keeps walking as though the water was not there at all. Not to mention that there was a storm in the midst of the sea to the point that the boat which held the disciples was shaking. Notice, we have a shaking boat and a walking Christ. Some will choose to stay the same and shake with the boat of religion that keeps us shaking in fear; others will choose to see that God is raising a corporate man and walk in alignment.

To say that we must do things the same way that we have "always" done them, is to say that once God gives a directive, or once we choose a path, God is not permitted to speak anything fresh to us. It is a shame that we have a 21st century condition of the world, but the church wants to continue with early 1900s methods which will not work in this society. We refuse to change because we fail to realize that whatever we are doing presently is the result of change. Do you really believe that the church in the 1500s used the same hymn books that you use now? Or that the saints of the 1200s used our methods of worship? Of course not! What happened then? There was a change. This change or revolution was the result of a revelation. As we come into revelation, we are expected to violently apply the revelation to our lives so that we experience a revolution that will make us more relative to the world in which we live. In order for us to experience the power of the kingdom of God, we must expediently embrace this great paradigm shift. All 2000 different denominations in America will tell you that they have to be different from the other denominations because of some form of truth that they have grasped. Now, I am certainly not saying that I agree with them, I am saying that is what they will tell you. While I am not totally opposed to denominations in the sense of belonging to a group of people who all rally around their doctrine, I am fully in favor of a breakdown of the denominational wall so that the whole nation can function together under one banner of The Kingdom of God.

Exodus 19:6, NKJV
6 And you shall be to Me a kingdom of priests and a holy nation. These are the words which you shall speak to the children of Israel.

1 Peter 2:9-10, NKJV
9 But you are a chosen generation, a royal priesthood, a holy nation, His own special people, that you may proclaim the praises of Him who called you out of darkness into His marvelous light; 10 who once were not a people but are now the people of God, who had not obtained mercy but now have obtained mercy.

"A fresh wind is indeed blowing . . . . To some the changes are refreshing breezes. For others, they are as fearsome as a hurricane."
—Episcopalian Bishop Barbara Harris

This general reference to change by Bishop Harris is very applicable to where the body of Christ is now. For many, change is not embraced nor celebrated because we are not generally a people who like transition. Yet, transitions are being made around us all the time. Twenty years ago it was normal to work in a certain career field for 30 or more years. Now, it is rarely heard of because we transition much more frequently. If this is true of the society around us, why is there such a challenge to change in the church, which must function in this altering society?

Allow me to share with you something that happened in my home a few years ago. I noticed in the earlier part of my marriage that my wife and I were eating quite frequently and as a result gaining weight. It finally dawned on me, that we would always get hungry when we sat on the couch. After investigating the situation, I discovered that our problem was a subliminal message that we needed to eradicate. At the time we lived in a rather small condominium. The couch was facing the television, but it was also facing the kitchen. Once I realized that this was the cause of the sudden hunger when sitting on the couch, I determined that the only answer was to change our rather nice setup in order to keep from eating so much so

I turned the couch and the television to face the opposite wall. I decided to make the change while my wife was on her way in from work because I always made it home from work before she did. When she walked in she discovered that what was one way when she left, was totally reconfigured when she returned. Needless to say, it took her a moment (a couple of days) to adjust. Once she embraced the change, she began to move the pictures on the walls around so as to complete the finishing touches necessary to make the adjustment more appealing to the eyes. When everything was done, we were able to sit on the couch and not have sudden hunger pains because the problematic issue was behind us.

The great challenge in the church is to come to the place where we allow our perception to change that we may put some things behind us and move forward. There is a glorious paradigm shift that is taking place; unfortunately, for many this great shift is not so glorious because they are blinded by the victories of past performances and cannot perceive that the old move may not be bringing present victory.

The Great Paradigm Shift involves nine major areas:
- Small traditional churches to mega-churches
- Churches named after men to Bible based names
- One man band to multiplicity of leadership
- Controlling deacons to apostolic order
- Male dominated to female incorporated
- Church building centered to Marketplace ministry
- Denominations to covenant connections
- Stained glass windows and pews to houses and sofas
- Struggling for survival Christians to gloriously reigning kings and priests

This book would be entirely too long if I attempted to exhaust information regarding every facet of the great paradigm shift. We will discuss all of these areas in very limited detail because all of these areas speak of one great shifting. This great shifting is that of divine oneness with God and man.

Ephesians 4:1-6, NKJV

1 I, therefore, the prisoner of the Lord, beseech you to walk worthy of the calling with which you were called, 2 with all lowliness and gentleness, with longsuffering, bearing with one another in love, 3 endeavoring to keep the unity of the Spirit in the bond of peace. 4 There is one body and one Spirit, just as you were called in one hope of your calling; 5 one Lord, one faith, one baptism; 6 one God and Father of all, who is above all, and through all, and in you all.

Sadly, the church as we know it is completely divided and is no better than when the Apostle Paul was pleading with the church at Ephesus to strive for unity. Thankfully, through the process of revelation and intercession, many leaders are beginning to bridge the many gaps among us and bring us to a fascinating place of tremendous oneness. Obstacles of individualism, humanism, socio-economic class, gender, ethnicity, and denominational barriers all work against the unity that we are to have in Christ exhibited as unity in fellowship, unity in spirit, and unity in faith.

Galatians 3:28, NKJV
28 There is neither Jew nor Greek, there is neither slave nor free, there is neither male nor female; for you are all one in Christ Jesus.

Some folks have even determined that they do not need to attend church at all because of the mass division that exists denominationally, the phony and sometimes even messy saints, and the egocentric showboating that is displayed through arrogant preachers who preach to impress one another as opposed to presenting relevant truth that changes lives. While all of the above are very much so real, I believe that there is a revolution that has begun and soon all of these things will still be real, REAL DEAD!

God has not ordained that individuals sit at home and watch televangelists referring to them as your TV-Pastor. I am not opposed to television preaching or radio teaching. As a matter of fact, I am not sure that we have enough of either. I am, however, completely opposed to the spirit of isolation and individualism, whether caused by past hurts in church or through a perpetual spirit of unwillingness to submit to authority. No doubt Jesus came to build his church, but what presently exists as the church may not be the equivalent of what he came to establish. In another chapter I will discuss the shift that is taking place in our understanding of marketplace ministry. For now, let me say that we all need to be part of a fellowship of believers for mutual edification.

Hebrews 10:25, NKJV
25 not forsaking the assembling of ourselves together, as is the manner of some, but exhorting one another, and so much the more as you see the Day approaching.

A simple understanding of this passage in Hebrews makes it clear that we need fellowship and must not deny its importance. Some ask, "What is the answer to all of this displacement and bewilderment in the body of Christ?" The answer lies in Covenant Community.

Covenant Community is not just a concept. It is rather a way of life. Every church must strive to go beyond convenient lives of Christianity to becoming a people who gather together under one vision which becomes the single heart of all that we say and do. We must cease to operate according to our individual, self-centered, and self-gratifying way of thinking and enter into a corporate, communal way of living which strengthens our individual destiny.

The word community is the combination of two words, "common" and "unity". Common is of Latin origin *communis*, belonging to the generality. Unity is from the Hebrew word *henotes*, oneness. Therefore, community is general oneness. This was the desire of the Apostle Paul in the entire book of Ephesians as well as is 1 Corinthians 12 and Philippians 2:1-4.

As we examine this way of life known as Covenant Community, we will discover that it is not a new concept to the world. If you read the introduction, you noted that the concept of community has its roots in the creation of mankind according to the book of Genesis. As we look at the rest of the world, outside of the church, we will notice that people all around us desire to be a part of a community.

One of the difficult nuisances of our day is that of gang violence. If we take a moment to look at gangs from a communal sense, we will have to note that each of the gangs is built as a community. This community is established through a mutual hatred for another group of individuals, who also form a community. The gang community is brought into oneness through a select color that represents the gang. Depending on the size numerically and the compass of their sphere or territory of rule, individuals may not know everyone within their "set", but they are able to recognize one another through a given hand gesture and/or color that is worn.

Fraternities and sororities also share a common purpose, colors and hand gestures to identify those who are a part of their community. In most cases, the fraternity or sorority often share an emblem that also classifies the community. Sometimes, people may perpetrate membership to one of these frats or sororities though association with someone who may be a legitimate member. Yet, this becomes apparent as a perpetration because the individual does not always know the secret hand gestures or ceremonial rites of passage.

Both of these examples demonstrate different types of relational communities. In both cases, individuals have various entitlements, recognitions, and a community in which one finds identity. Again, the members may not know one another personally, but through various agents of identification the members are able to recognize one another. Oftentimes, people love to be associated with a gang, fraternity, sorority, or any other type of identifying community because of the advantages that come with the association. I remember sitting back watching the movie "Legally Blonde 2" with my wife and son one evening. As we watched, we noticed the struggle that Elle was having with getting Bruiser's legislative bill to become a serious topic of discussion in Congress. It was not until Elle noted that she had a connection with a very powerful woman in Congress that a glimpse of hope became apparent. Now, the woman who would not take Elle seriously takes a personal interest in Elle's agenda because she takes a personal interest in Elle. Not only is there a coming together communally with this woman but Elle also finds another association with a powerful man in Congress. The two discover that they both have gay dogs who have taken a liking to each other. Now that they have found common ground, the two begin to take interest in one another's purposes for being in Washington. Ultimately, Elle's bill is not only taken seriously but it passes in Congress. Why? She found herself involved in common unity which opened the door for her need to be met.

My understanding of community was greatly influenced while I worked at Texas Wesleyan University as the Resident Director in charge of three dormitories. One of my first assignments upon the return of the students after the summer break was to introduce the 6 I's of Community taken from BASIC Model Programming at Miami University in Ohio. The model states the following:

1. Communities must receive a formal Introduction. New students are unfamiliar with physical surroundings, policies, and practices. Older members of community are responsible for welcoming, orienting, and teaching norms; values and rules of community introductions to community may be formal programs or informal discussions and observations.

2. Communities should provide opportunities for Interaction. Provides residents opportunities to share common experiences = bonding as students interact. They are exposed to different levels of development, knowledge and experience, which allow them to both learn and teach. Ideally, staff, faculty, and students participate in these common experience = promotes a feeling of campus as a community.

3. Communities must seek resident Involvement. A true community encourages, expects, and rewards broad-based member involvement. Environment is characterized by a high degree of interaction with students assuming a multitude of roles. Everyone is needed and important. High involving floors are characterized by supportive interactions with students naturally helping one another with personal and academic concerns and issues.

4. Communities must allow residents to have Influence. Control is vested in members and students exert maximum control over their physical and social environments. Students are expected to develop a social contract whereby group standards are affirmed both individually and collectively. In such communities students feel important, their perspective is valued, and their contributions are essential to the welfare of the group.

5. Communities must create, among residents, a sense of Investment. Investment is a reflection of psychological ownership flows naturally from influence and involvement institutional or group property is guarded and protected rather than damaged students understand and appreciate the need for open, honest and assertive communication with one another.

6. Community members must share a sense of Identity. Students have shared symbols much like fraternities and sororities. Members describe themselves in collective terms such as we and us not I and them.

No doubt we can see many ways that these six I's can be used in the church. Some aspects include introduction through New Member Orientation, interaction through in-house ministries and cell groups, investment through time, talent, and treasure and a revelatory understanding of our identity in Christ. Needless to say, there is a plethora of other ways that these can be implemented in the church through fellowship. I pray that covenant communities will begin praying for strategies as to how to utilize this model.

Luke 16:8, KJV

8 And the lord commended the unjust steward, because he had done wisely: for the children of this world are in their generation wiser than the children of light.

If the children of this world are able to come together in community and open doors for one another, how much more should we who have been brought together by the Blood come together as a true covenant community. We should be the model of community because we have a greater covenant than the rest of the world. Sadly, this is not the case within most churches because we have our own ideologies and agendas which keep us in warfare with one another. This warfare perpetuates spirits of division and manipulation, which we will discuss in greater detail in chapter 4. To combat this problematic mentality in the church, men and women of God who serve in headship must begin to proclaim unity and keep the concept of covenant community before the eyes and in the ears of its local parishioners. There must be a revolution that is the result of this revelation to bring us into a new place in the Kingdom of God whereby we will be able to bring down the works of the devil and manifest the fullness of our glorious Christ in the world. Whether the fellowship is in a building with pews and a steeple or in a house with a garage and sofas, we must get away from the Lord being "my shepherd", which he is, and cleave to a greater degree of truth that He is in fact "Our Father." When this happens, there will be a glorious unveiling of true covenant community which ushers in the revealing of the manifestation of the sons of God, whom the whole world is waiting to see come forth. No longer will be sheep in need of the protection of the shepherd but we will advance to being sons who receive our identity from the Father.

CHAPTER 2

The Nature of Covenant Communities

God is raising apostolic and prophetic voices in this hour to bring the body of Christ together as a covenant community, locally and globally. This holy assembly of the saints of God in the body of Christ is not merely a relational community as was discussed in chapter one. Covenant communities are not merely the coming together of individuals, but a people integrated into Christ which strengthens the impact and influence of Christ in the world. The power of the true covenant community lays within the force that brings us all together, the blood of Christ.

Ephesians 2:12-13, NIV
12 remember that at that time you were separate from Christ, excluded from citizenship in Israel and foreigners to the covenants of the promise, without hope and without God in the world. 13 But now in Christ Jesus you who once were far away have been brought near through the blood of Christ.

For years I have heard the figurative expression, "Blood is thicker than water." For those who are not familiar with this statement, it is generally used when comparing family relationships with any other type of relationship. If the expression is true in its context, then we must understand that our position in Christ is greater than our position in our biological family because we have been brought together by both blood and water.

1 John 5:6-8, NKJV
6 This is He who came by water and blood—Jesus Christ; not only by water, but by water and blood. And it is the Spirit who bears witness, because the Spirit is

truth. 7 For there are three that bear witness in heaven: the Father, the Word, and the Holy Spirit; and these three are one. 8 And there are three that bear witness on earth: the Spirit, the water, and the blood; and these three agree as one.

Let's recap momentarily the first covenant community. The Bible says that God created the community by taking woman out of the side of man because it was not good for man to be alone, "all-one". This was necessary because Adam needed someone to help him release through multiplication the global covenant community that was to become mankind. If we take this event and couple it with 1 John 5, then we will discover that they come together to form a mighty truth.

John 19:34
34 But one of the soldiers pierced His side with a spear, and immediately blood and water came out.

What is the significance of blood and water coming out of the pierced side? This single act brings us back to general oneness, covenant community. I believe that just as God opened the side of man to let the woman out of man, God, through the soldier, had to once again open the man, Christ, to let the woman, the church, back in. Now, in Christ it is good for man to be all-one. This is the powerful expression of the passion of Christ in His garden as he affirms his oneness with the Father and intercedes for our place in that oneness that he and the Father share.

John 17:9-11, 15-24
*9 I pray for them. I do not pray for the world but for those whom You have given Me, for they are Yours. 10 And all Mine are Yours, and Yours are Mine, and **I am glorified in them**. 11 Now I am no longer in the world, but these are in the world, and I come to You. Holy Father, keep through Your name those whom You have given Me, **that they may be one** as We are.*

*15 I do not pray that You should take them out of the world, but that You should keep them from the evil one. 16 They are not of the world, just as I am not of the world. 17 Sanctify them by Your truth. Your word is truth. 18 As You sent Me into the world, I also have sent them into the world. 19 And for their sakes I sanctify Myself, that they also may be sanctified by the truth. 20 I do not pray for these alone, but also for those who will believe in Me through their word; 21 **that they all may be one**, as You, Father, are in Me, and I in You; **that they also may be one in Us**, that the world may believe that You sent Me. 22 And the glory which You gave Me I have given them, **that they may be one just as We are one**: 23 I in them, and You in Me; **that they may be made perfect in one**, and that the world may know that You have* *sent Me, and have loved them as You have loved Me. 24 Father, I desire that they also whom You gave Me may be with Me where I am, that they may behold My glory which You have given Me; for You loved Me before the foundation of the world.*

The above prayer of Jesus is the central focal point of this book. While we will look further into this powerful prayer and highlight various areas of interesting truths, at this point I want us to understand that covenant community is the heartbeat of Jesus. Just as it is his passionate desire that we be one, it should equally be a driving force among us.

Many will read this book and argue that my call, which is the call of many and more importantly the call of God, for oneness in the body of Christ will do nothing more than create further divisions of presently fragmented churches and denominations. Allow me to say, this book is not a call to another denomination but rather to a holy nation under the banner of the Kingdom of God, locally and globally. We are called to be one in Him. Every leader should require this understanding within the local church as well as maintain submission to this way of life in respect to the global community. When the sense of covenant community is restored in the body of Christ, our influence will break through minimal parameters and cause us to impact the world in a much greater way because we will all speak with uniformity.

The concept of a covenant community is one of the most challenging aspects of the Kingdom walk in this vast, individualistic society in which we live. Yet, the truth remains that we must be converted from this primarily individualistic mode of thought to a corporate way of life. Consequently, leadership is challenged to constantly plant the notion of covenant community before the people that they may inscribe it upon their hearts. The mentality of Israel, as it is depicted in the twenty-fourth chapter of Exodus, insists that covenant community is an essential element in accomplishing the assignments that God gives to headship who in turn communicates the assignment to the people.

Exodus 24:1-3, NKJV
1 Now He said to Moses, "Come up to the Lord, you and Aaron, Nadab and Abihu, and seventy of the elders of Israel, and worship from afar. 2 And Moses alone shall come near the Lord, but they shall not come near; nor shall the people go up with him." So Moses came and told the people all the words of the Lord and all the judgments. And all the people answered with one voice and said, "All the words which the Lord has said we will do."

The previous verses reveal several truths that must be understood as we transition from the mindset of individuals with church membership to becoming a covenant community. First, the call of God is for Moses and his leadership to come up to the Lord. The call of a covenant community is a call to a higher place whereby truth is revealed in a dimension beyond church as we traditionally know it. In this hour, leadership must be free to be God-ward. The traditional church member mentality is one that keeps the pastor busy with menial tasks that produce pitiful warmed over sermons ending in mediocre members. For those who are not interested in becoming all that God has ordained and find contentment in the mundane, a true covenant community is probably not the place to be desired. A true covenant community will have fresh vision that will provoke the community to action. The man or woman of God that is in the place of headship within the covenant community must be free to seek the Lord that he or she may walk fully in revelation. When revelation and illumination come together it brings forth inspiration for the extermination of ignorance through violent application, which fosters transformation that ultimately leads to one's elevation.

Secondly, Moses obeyed God. This fact brings us to the place of Theocracy and away from Democracy. The church as we know it is filled with individual ideas, idiosyncrasies and self-centered agendas, which have no relevance in the Kingdom of God. A covenant community must always propagate the reality that the government of the community is not ruled by men, but by God alone. Furthermore, it is on this premise of truth that we see Moses returning to the people who are gathered together to hear what God has to say through the leader. Beloved, we do not gather to debate personal feelings, but rather we gather as community to bow to the banner of righteousness as a covenant people. As we understand the principle of covenant community, we will accomplish the latter clause of Exodus 24, a*nd all the people answered with one voice and said, "All the words which the Lord has said we will do."*

Set ministry, in most cases known as the pastor, is responsible for clearly communicating the vision of the house. God is not in the business of releasing vision to a committee, although some seem to believe that He is. Rather God summons the leader up to his presence where he births vision in the heart of his selected, sent and set leader, and everyone who is placed by the Lord within the community will somehow fit and serve the vision of the house. While meeting the needs of the sheep of the pasture, set ministry must remain sensitive to the voice of God and not become preoccupied with just meeting the needs of the members. Having said that, we must comprehend that as leaders we are not called to use the people to build our communities, on the contrary we must equip the people in our communities to fulfill their destinies. The house must be exposed to all five facets of Ephesians 4:11 ministries to bring proper maturation.

Ephesians 4:11-14, KJV
11 And he gave some, apostles; and some, prophets; and some, evangelists; and some, pastors and teachers; 12 For the perfecting of the saints, for the work of the ministry, for the edifying of the body of Christ: 13 Till we all come in the unity of the

faith, and of the knowledge of the Son of God, unto a perfect man, unto the measure of the stature of the fullness of Christ: 14 That we henceforth be no more children, tossed to and fro, and carried about with every wind of doctrine, by the sleight of men, and cunning craftiness, whereby they lie in wait to deceive.

Whether the church is large or small, the bottom line is to accomplish the vision given by the set man and impact the sphere or circle of influence in which you are assigned. Every church will not be a mega-church. While there are many mega-ministries throughout the globe, each community must be careful not to enter into competition propagated by jealousy and envy. First of all, just because a ministry is large does not necessarily mean that the ministry is successful in the eyes of the Father. Before I say more concerning mega-ministries, allow me to say that some mega-ministries have received a bad reputation undeservingly. In some cases, this reputation is deserved, but that certainly is not the case for all. Many times the reputation of a mega church is tainted by those who are not members of the church. People on the outside must endeavor to refrain from speaking against ministries of which they are not intimately acquainted. Furthermore, as mentioned earlier, the idle gossip against a large ministry is sadly propagated by a spirit of jealousy and/or selfishness by ministers of significantly smaller ministries. If we must resort to foolish tactics of bashing popular ministry gifts to validate ourselves, then we have only further reinforced the reality that our ministries will remain and should remain in a constant state of mediocrity. Lastly, the media certainly should not be trusted in revealing truth to us regarding mega-ministries. Often times the media will oversimplify or "biggie size" an issue to make the story more compelling. In a later chapter we will seek to dispel this and other types of community cripplers.

No true covenant community has to remain small. As a matter of fact, one may go as far as to say that when a ministry is a true covenant community, ultimately the gifts and talents that are resident within the covenant community will begin to be recognized and utilized to impact cities, regions, and even nations. When this begins to happen within a local house, it will cease to be a small ministry in terms of impact. When this impact and influence begins to fully blossom, there is a great possibility that the ministry will ultimately become what we consider to be a mega church.

Acts 2:41-47, NKJV

41 Then those who gladly received His word were baptized; and that day about three thousand souls were added to them. 42 And they continued steadfastly in the apostles' doctrine and fellowship, in the breaking of bread, and in prayers. 43 Then fear came upon every soul, and many wonders and signs were done through the apostles. 44 Now all who believed were together, and had all things in common, 45 and sold their possessions and goods, and divided them among all, as anyone had need. 46 So continuing daily with one accord in the temple, and breaking bread from house to house, they ate their food with gladness and simplicity of heart, 47 praising God and having favor with all the people. And the Lord added to the church daily those who were being saved.

If we use the inception of the New Testament church from Acts 2 as a model, we will see that the church is intended to reach many. Some have gone as far as to say that all churches are supposed to be large and if they are not then they should close their doors because they are ineffective. I do not support this idea because I believe that each ministry, that is a true ministry, will grow in time as knowledge, revelation, vision, and gifting is increased. No true covenant community, however, should desire to remain small although the requirements are sometimes fewer with small ministries. If the community is truly changing lives, then there should be a strong desire to see other lives changed because of the anointing of the community. If this type of desire begins to flow from the constituents of the community and people on the outside begin to see the impact of the ministry on the lives of those within, then it will not be long before the small church begins to blossom and flourish. Again, I want to stress the fact that we are not to strive for mega-size but the order of God which fosters mega-covenant. As covenant remains our focus and drive, we perpetually live in a state of rest and allow God to add to the church such as are being saved and, of those who fit our vision and purpose, add to our community.

A mega-ministry should equate a mega-vision that will reach masses of people for the Kingdom of God. One of the advantages of a mega-ministry that operates in covenant community is the ability to generate wealth to support missions across the globe and impact the lives of those within their immediate setting. These finances also enable the influence of larger ministries to utilize venues such as television and radio to advance the gospel of the Kingdom of God.

Another advantage of mega-churches is the ability to have plurality of leadership. When there is plurality of leadership within a house, the senior pastor or set man is not overdriven. A worn out leader is not good for a covenant community. As men and women of God, we must understand that God has equipped our covenant community with individuals of gifting and abilities, thus we must perceive and confirm, in proper timing, grace on the lives of others to aid in leading the covenant community. As influence and impact increases through proper vision, so must the delegation of authority as we will see with Pastor Moses.

Exodus 18:17-21, NIV
17 Moses' father-in-law replied, "What you are doing is not good. 18 You and these people who come to you will only wear yourselves out. The work is too heavy

for you; you cannot handle it alone. 19 Listen now to me and I will give you some advice, and may God be with you. You must be the people's representative before God and bring their disputes to Him. 20 Teach them the decrees and laws, and show them the way to live and the duties they are to perform. 21 But select capable men from all the people—men who fear God, trustworthy men who hate dishonest gain—and appoint them as officials over thousands, hundreds, fifties and tens."

In the 1970s and 1980s, this concept was not fully embraced for various reasons. However, in the 21st century we cannot afford to have the one man band mentality. As the covenant community grows, the delegation of authority must be broadened. This will enable the set man to keep his or her face towards God. God must have the set man's undivided attention because the vision and revelation is to continue developing for greater influence and impact within the covenant community and beyond.

Many struggle in the body of Christ as the community experiences growth, declaring over and over that they do not desire to be a part of a large ministry because of the inability to get close to the set ministry. The reality is that we must stay out of the trap of immature and selfish mentalities such as this. To help with this process of community development we must seek along with the set ministry to promote the growth of the body as membership leans on one another for strength and development and not leadership exclusively.

Ephesians 4:15-16, KJV

15 But speaking the truth in love, may grow up into Him in all things, which is the head, even Christ: 16 From whom the whole body fitly joined together and compacted by that which every joint supplieth, according to the effectual working in the measure of every part, maketh increase of the body unto the edifying of itself in love.

The missing ingredient in many ministries regardless of size is the element of love. Throughout the scriptures, love is portrayed as the overarching force that holds the covenant community together. Everyone in the community must understand their responsibility to generate and maintain healthy relationships that are grounded in love. Everything we do must cause our love, one for the other, to ever increase that all may see the height and depth of our love for God and for one another.

John 13:34-35, NKJV

34 A new commandment I give to you, that you love one another; as I have loved you, that you also love one another. 35 By this all will know that you are My disciples, if you have love for one another."

Love is the logo of the covenant community. Our love is to be visible and speak the sentiments of the heart of our ministries. This love is not to be anything like what the world calls love. Covenant communities must have the understanding that our love is for God and man. Some are focused on God alone, but the true covenant community must comprehend that love for God means loving men and that loving men remains strong and develops greater as we love God. As we consider the various types of love, phileo and agape speak to the type of love that is needed in the covenant community. Phileo is brotherly love, and agape is unconditional love. When phileo and agape come together, we become a glorious demonstration of the Kingdom of God.

1 John 4:7-13, NKJV
Beloved, let us love one another, for love is of God; and everyone who loves is born of God and knows God. 8 He who does not love does not know God, for God is love. 9 In this the love of God was manifested toward us, that God has sent His only begotten Son into the world, that we might live through Him. 10 In this is love, not that we loved God, but that He loved us and sent His Son to be the propitiation for our sins. 11 Beloved, if God so loved us, we also ought to love one another. 12 No one has seen God at any time. If we love one another, God abides in us, and His love has been perfected in us. 13 By this we know that we abide in Him, and He in us, because He has given us of His Spirit.

The true covenant community loves unconditionally as the family of God. The very nature of God is love. Consequently, if we are going to be the church of the living God, then our love must be alive and well. Our love is to be unchangeable and unmovable. This is what the Apostle Paul commended the churches in Philippi and Thessalonica for, their ever abounding love.

Philippians 1:9, NKJV
9 And this I pray that your love may abound still more and more in knowledge and all discernment.

1 Thessalonians 3:12, NKJV
12 And may the Lord make you increase and abound in love to one another and to all, just as we do to you.

What a great place the covenant community becomes when our members understand that they are in a house of abounding love! This certainly does not sound like the traditional churches that existed when I was a child. The saints seemingly loved to embarrass one another for their areas of shortcoming. Seems to me, the covenant community should be the safest place to live without feeling inadequate. Every person should be made to feel that they are absolutely vital to the community. Why is this necessary? Because every person is important to the community. Every person should be the giver and recipient of abounding love. This love is not exhibited as the saints march around the church and hug one another during the worship celebration. On the contrary, this type of love is demonstrated at its finest when someone is able to confess their fault to another member of the community and not be the recipient of judgment but affection. This love demonstrates its power by embracing the individual holistically without ever holding their sin over their head. As a child I remember hearing over and over that prayer availeth much. As a young adult I began to understand that prayer is powerful in and of itself, but it is the effectual fervent prayer that avails much. When singleness of heart is reached, our prayers cease to be prayers of pity and woe; they become prayers of passion and fire.

James 5:16, KJV
16 Confess your faults one to another, and pray one for another, that ye may be healed. The effectual fervent prayer of a righteous man availeth much.

The powerful truth of James 5 is that while many saints of God believe that their life is void of fault and imperfection, James encourages the saints to recognize their faults and not live with fear of the unfavorable opinion of others. Every child of God must have someone in their life in which they may confide. The bi-product of this type of atmosphere is the healing balm of Christ. The challenge now is the willingness to trust one another enough to reach out and touch someone else's life and allow someone to reach out and touch you when you are strong while they are weak.

Ecclesiastes 4:9-10, NKJV
9 Two are better than one, because they have a good reward for their labor. 10 For if they fall, one will lift up his companion. But woe to him who is alone when he falls, for he has no one to help him up.

CHAPTER 3

Reach Out and Touch Someone

If we perceive the word of God correctly, we must all conclude that the Bible is in fact a book of covenant. The first and last books of the Old Testament (New King James Version) use the term covenant and the first and last books of the New Testament use the term covenant. I do not believe this to be by chance, but by way of significance. As a matter of fact, the word covenant is literally used 335 times within the corridors of scripture (NKJV) and is referred to indirectly frequently. Perhaps as we see the words Old Testament and New Testament we can see the word testament itself is the Greek word diatheékees, which means covenant.

While covenant is the underlying theme of scripture, it does not seem to be at the forefront of our desire in the church. Ironically, we talk about covenant but we see very little of it in manifestation within the modern day church. Covenant between men in scripture involved their very livelihood, whereas, our menial definition of covenant involves sitting next to someone at church for two hours with the only contact being an occasional high-five and an instructed cold and shallow hug to welcome one another to the service.

2 Kings 2:1-13, NKJV

1 And it came to pass, when the LORD was about to take up Elijah into heaven by a whirlwind, that Elijah went with Elisha from Gilgal. 2 Then Elijah said to Elisha, "Stay here, please, for the LORD has sent me on to Bethel." But Elisha said, "As the LORD lives, and as your soul lives, I will not leave you!" So they went down to Bethel. 3 Now the sons of the prophets who were at Bethel came out to Elisha, and said to him, "Do you know that the LORD will take away your master from over you today?" And he said, "Yes, I know; keep silent!" 4 Then Elijah said to him,

"Elisha, stay here, please, for the LORD has sent me on to Jericho." But he said, "As the LORD lives, and as your soul lives, I will not leave you!" So they came to Jericho. 5 Now the sons of the prophets who were at Jericho came to Elisha and said to him, "Do you know that the LORD will take away your master from over you today?"

So he answered, "Yes, I know; keep silent!" 6 Then Elijah said to him, "Stay here, please, for the LORD has sent me on to the Jordan." But he said, "As the LORD lives, and as your soul lives, I will not leave you!" So the two of them went on. 7 And fifty men of the sons of the prophets went and stood facing them at a distance, while the two of them stood by the Jordan. 8 Now Elijah took his mantle, rolled it up, and struck the water; and it was divided this way and that, so that the two of them crossed over on dry ground. 9 And so it was, when they had crossed over, that Elijah said to Elisha, "Ask! What may I do for you, before I am taken away from you?" Elisha said, "Please let a double portion of your spirit be upon me." 10 So he said, "You have asked a hard thing. Nevertheless, if you see me when I am taken from you, it shall be so for you; but if not, it shall not be so." 11 Then it happened, as they continued on and talked, that suddenly a chariot of fire appeared with horses of fire, and separated the two of them; and Elijah went up by a whirlwind into heaven. 12 And Elisha saw it, and he cried out, "My father, my father, the chariot of Israel and its horsemen!" So he saw him no more. And he took hold of his own clothes and tore them into two pieces. 13 He also took up the mantle of Elijah that had fallen from him, and went back and stood by the bank of the Jordan.

Dr. Mark Hanby, has frequently declared, "Father-son order is the order of God within His Kingdom." The concept of father-son order has at its very roots, covenant. One of the most recognizable and purest forms of father-son order is that of Elijah and Elisha. So strong was the covenant that Elijah could not get rid of Elisha after three failed attempts to do so because it was Elijah's mantle not his handouts that interested Elisha. Spiritual sons must come to the place that they are so interested in receiving the generational blessing that they are void of offense. Elisha not only endured the attempts of Elijah to leave him behind, but he also fought off the attempts of other sons of the prophets to change his heart towards Elijah. True sons like Elisha recognize, as did the disciples of Jesus, that their father has the word of life for them.

John 6:67-68, KJV
67 Then said Jesus unto the twelve, "Will ye also go away"? 68 Then Simon Peter answered him, "Lord, to whom shall we go? Thou hast the words of eternal life."

It is important to understand that in every covenant community there are those who desire to be true sons and daughters and then there are those who are just a part of the multitude. The multitude is made up of those who are following for the fish and the loaves, otherwise known as slammin' choirs, entertaining preachers, or even business opportunity adventures. Every set ministry gift must be careful to accurately identify the agenda of those who follow so as to not exhaust your energy with the multitude to the neglect of true sons and daughters. True fathers are able to use wisdom in testing the commitment of those who follow. To some, this may appear uncouth, but this is exactly what Elijah and Jesus did to challenge their followers to come to the next level. They created a situation where their followers had to internally judge their true commitment to the ministry gift. Those who bail where never fully persuaded internally that the set ministry gift was their true spiritual leader. Those who remain will see you and recognize you as Elisha recognized Elijah as "my father, my father".

1 John 2:19, NKJV
19 They went out from us, but they were not of us; for if they had been of us, they would have continued with us; but they went out that they might be made manifest, that none of them were of us.

Be it understood, no covenant community is perfect in terms of being void of confrontational uprisings from time to time. There will be challenges and situations that must be worked through with wisdom. Due to the inevitability of disappointment in every ministry, it is important that set ministry remains confident in the gifting and grace of God that is on his/her life.

Exodus 32:25-26, NKJV
25 Now when Moses saw that the people were unrestrained (for Aaron had not restrained them, to their shame among their enemies), 26 then Moses stood in the entrance of the camp, and said, "Whoever is on the LORD's side—come to me!" And all the sons of Levi gathered themselves together to him.

Moses demonstrates for those of us in set ministry how we are to remain confident in the great God of glory regardless of the condition of the people and those whom Moses left in leadership as he went up to the mountain. As you read the entire 32nd chapter of Exodus you will discover that the people have begun losing confidence in Moses while he is away with God.

Aaron was left with the responsibility of leading the people as Moses would; however, Aaron gave in to the requests of the people to create their own god. Upon Moses' return, he finds the community in complete disarray and uproar. It is such a mess that Joshua brings to Moses' attention that the noise sounds like a war cry. Upon discovering the happenings of the people, Moses is challenged with the feelings of disappointment in Aaron and the people. As we begin to understand that disappointment is inevitable, we will ultimately respond as

Moses with sheer confidence in God and his ability to use us in leadership. Had Moses given up as a result of Aaron's lack of leadership in this situation, he would have missed the opportunity to raise Joshua as his successor.

Covenant, however is not just father to son. We must also perceive covenant as brother to brother if we are to have a true covenant community. One of the most noted covenant relationships was that of David and Jonathan.

1 Samuel 18:1-4, NKJV
1 Now when he had finished speaking to Saul, the soul of Jonathan was knit to the soul of David, and Jonathan loved him as his own soul. 2 Saul took him that day, and would not let him go home to his father's house anymore. 3 Then Jonathan and David made a covenant, because he loved him as his own soul. 4 And Jonathan took off the robe that was on him and gave it to David, with his armor, even to his sword and his bow and his belt.

The relationship between David and Jonathan was so great in the spirit that Jonathan was willing to protect David even from his natural father, Saul. This demonstrates the true power of covenant, as Jonathan puts his entire livelihood on the line. If anyone had reason to not like David or not be concerned about David's well-being it was Jonathan. Jonathan demonstrates his lack of fear of David and reckons him to be one with Jonathan through the exchange of garments. David is said of Jonathan to be one soul with him. Covenant goes beyond mere lip service; it involves the exchange of life. Many have clearly stated that a contract is signed in ink while a covenant is signed in blood.

As we will explore further in a later chapter, this powerful covenant could not be more clearly seen than in the death of our innocent substitute, the spotless lamb, who will die on the cross and exchange his life for ours. Because the cross is both vertical and horizontal, we are able to see that Jesus came to unite us as one with God and with men. This type of covenantal love enables us to fulfill the law of Christ that we love God and love our neighbor as we love ourselves.

Romans 12:15
15 Rejoice with those who rejoice, and weep with those who weep.

As the covenant community develops, it is important that we maintain singleness of heart. While many are busy competing with those around to keep up with the status quo, it is imperative that we remember that we are called to complement and live corporately in harmony with one another. The community is no place for rivalry and disharmony perpetuated by competition and other self-centered behaviors. The community should be the one place however, where everyone receives compassion when necessary and shares celebration for victories achieved. While all events, good or bad, do not warrant the entire community's participation, there should be connections that have been made with those of like precious faith within the community that none have to weep alone nor rejoice alone. As we learn to weep and rejoice together, we establish an amalgamation that is not easily shaken.

In this time of individualism and self-gratification, a good dose of brotherly love that breeds a sense of belonging for all who are added by the Lord is quite refreshing when it is done without ulterior motive. Those who God joins to the house should be cared for in the best way possible. The community that learns to share in one another's successes and failures is the one that will experience great victories and will endure the test of time.

This principle is certainly true in the family which is also a type of covenant community. In marriage counseling sessions, the term submission generally comes up from the man who desires his fiancé to be one who submits to him. Immediately I draw attention to his need to make his fiancé feel secure. Submission is the bi-product of security. If she doesn't feel secure with the man, then she will have a difficult time coming into submission to him. The same is true of the covenant community. As we learn to make people feel secure as opposed to ignoring their pain and downplaying their triumphs, we will subsequently create an atmosphere of submission and coalition.

James 5:14,16

14 Is anyone among you sick? Let him call for the elders of the church, and let them pray over him, anointing him with oil in the name of the Lord.

16 Confess your trespasses to one another, and pray for one another, that you may be healed. The effective, fervent prayer of a righteous man avails much.

The confession of one's trespasses is only feasible in its purest form when an atmosphere of submission and coalition has been established. While there are those circles that have utilized various types of confessionals for their parishioners, I believe that this type of confession referred to in James 4:16 should be done voluntarily, subsequent to finding a fellow believer that can be trusted to handle what will be revealed. In the old church, we had the mentality of marching individuals down the aisles to confess certain sins. This however, is not wisdom. Individuals should be able to find those within the community who are able to bear their burden and handle their issues. Order is maintained by the apostle as he instructs the saints to call for the elders of the church that they may pray over them. Many have argued that this is not necessary because people can get a prayer through for themselves. I do not want to argue that point, as I do not believe that it was the apostle's agenda to make the people dependent on the clergy. I do however believe that his motive is clear; create an atmosphere of mutual edification and submission. As this begins to happen, the saints develop a strong sense of connection and love for one another that they are able to enter into a deeper, fervent prayer life that does not center solely on themselves, but for all who are of the household of faith.

Galatians 6:1-2,10 NKJV

1 Brethren, if a man is overtaken in any trespass, you who are spiritual restore such a one in a spirit of gentleness, considering yourself lest you also be tempted. 2 Bear one another's burdens, and so fulfill the law of Christ.

10 Therefore, as we have opportunity, let us do good to all, especially to those who are of the household of faith.

What is the missing element in many covenant communities? Compassion. The covenant community should be so filled with compassion that we are not afraid to reach out and touch one another. Compassion enables believers to find solace from one another by dispelling competition and arrogance. This must remain evident in the pulpit and in the pews. While I am not saying that believers should be allowed to remain in the elementary school of their Christian experience, I do however believe that all of us need someone to reach out and touch us where we need to be reached and not just reminded of our weaknesses. Let us be guilty of not allowing individuals within our communities to experience the dreadful plague of their heart as they confront overwhelming perplexities in isolation. We must make the conscious effort to display the compassionate love of Christ to those who are in need of our compassion, comfort, and covenant. After all, God comforts us in our tribulation so that we are qualified and capable of providing comfort for others.

2 Corinthians 1:3-4, NKJV

3 Blessed be the God and Father of our Lord Jesus Christ, the Father of mercies and God of all comfort, 4 who comforts us in all our tribulation, that we may be able to comfort those who are in any trouble, with the comfort with which we ourselves are comforted by God.

As we partake in this holy realm of brotherhood, we will discover a powerful anointing that flows through us, enabling and empowering us to give strength to those who are weak and comfort to those that mourn. This takes us beyond the comfort zone of convenient personal Christianity into a glorious realm of covenant community that requires us to do more than just say, "I am praying for you." Rather we come to the place where we say, "I see you and am willing to lay down my life long enough to use my strength to cover your weakness and minister to your wounds. God has raised me to apply bandages and balm to your place of pain." Jesus again becomes our ultimate example as he is seen in many instances touching lives.

Matthew 20:33-34

33 They said to Him, "Lord, that our eyes may be opened." 34 So Jesus had compassion and touched their eyes. And immediately their eyes received sight, and they followed Him.

Mark 1:41

41 Then Jesus, moved with compassion, stretched out His hand and touched him, and said to him, "I am willing; be cleansed."

As we learn this principle we are able to empower the community to build-up those who are a part of our fellowship as well as those who are on the outside of the temple. The tender heart reveals itself to the one from whom it expects relief. We will never be able to touch issues that the world or our community members do not trust to reveal to us. In both cases of Matthew and Mark, Jesus did not remind them that they had a need, nor did he use his knowledge of their condition to ridicule them. On the contrary, he recognized their desire for relief and allowed himself to be moved with compassion, which ultimately produced their healing. This is not just another action of Jesus to celebrate but rather to duplicate.

1 Peter 3:8-9

8 Finally, all of you be of one mind, having compassion for one another; love as brothers, be tenderhearted, be courteous; 9 not returning evil for evil or reviling for reviling, but on the contrary blessing, knowing that you were called to this, that you may inherit a blessing.

This was not just some irrelevant rhetoric from Peter rather it was the heartbeat of his conviction. He fully understood the power of compassion and demonstration of Holy Ghost power. Sometimes the giver of compassion must be able to see more than the direct object of the request that the true need may be met as opposed to reinforcing a constant need resulting from the wrong mentality.

Acts 3:3-9

3 Who, seeing Peter and John about to go into the temple, asked for alms. 4 And fixing his eyes on him, with John, Peter said, "Look at us." 5 So he gave them his attention, expecting to receive something from them. 6 Then Peter said, "Silver and gold I do not have, but what I do have I give you: In the name of Jesus Christ of Nazareth, rise up and walk." 7 And he took him by the right hand and lifted him up, and immediately his feet and ankle bones received strength. 8 So he, leaping up, stood and walked and entered the temple with them—walking, leaping, and praising God. 9 And all the people saw him walking and praising God.

Before closing this chapter, I want us to consider that the church has a great need to touch Christ. Sometimes we can become so satisfied with the status quo and a complacent existence that we fail to see that we ourselves are in need of healing. Through a parade of choir robes, convention pumps, tailored suits, and Washington possessed pocketbooks for offering, we cover up the reality of true issues within our walls that keep us perpetually ill and this condition is stopping life from having an opportunity of conception. Before anyone will be able to touch the church and receive healing, the church must receive wholeness and out of that wholeness, virtue will flow.

Matthew 9:20-21, NKJV
20 And suddenly, a woman who had a flow of blood for twelve years came from behind and touched the hem of His garment. 21 For she said to herself, "If only I may touch His garment, I shall be made well."

At Hope of Glory, we have learned to view the scriptures from a holistic, Kingdom perspective rather than a mere need oriented, church standpoint. I have come to believe that the woman of Matthew 9 speaks of the church. She has had an issue of blood for twelve years. The constant flow of blood, if you look at a natural woman, disables a woman from reproducing. She is unable to bear children. Does this sound like any churches that you know? They've been around for a long time but their issues are stopping them from receiving the true seed of the word to bring forth sons and daughters. The cry of her heart was simply to touch the hem of His garment that she may be made well. May I say to the church, it is time that we reach out and touch Him that we be made well! Ironically, this woman understood something else of great significance. She understood that she didn't have to go for his head, just touch the hem of His garment. Perhaps she read about this somewhere!

Psalm 133:1-2
1 Behold, how good and how pleasant it is for brethren to dwell together in unity! 2 It is like the precious oil upon the head, running down on the beard, the beard of Aaron, running down on the edge of his garments.

The reality is that while many are jockeying for headship positions in the church, what we really need are some good skirts. If the head of the community is truly anointed, then those who are in alignment will receive and maintain the residue that flows from Aaron's beard. So many churches are being split because of the strong desire of many for attention and recognition. Perhaps you may feel insignificant to the body, however, understand that the corporate man can not move unless he is properly covered, just as you don't go anywhere until you are in appropriate attire. When everyone falls in place and proper alignment, the world can reach out and touch the saints of the community and find healing. This is why God has raised up apostles, prophets, and others to bring the body of Christ into a greater place of maturity. If we spend all of our time healing one another over and over again, when will we have the time and energy to heal those who are sick on the outside of our four walls? There must be a realm that we can access where the covenant community is not just a hospital for the saints. Perhaps there is a dimension that we can access whereby the saints receive wholeness that cause them to cease being the patients and become the doctors and nurses for those who are on the outside waiting for the bed that has been occupied for the last twelve years.

Genesis 49:13, NKJV
13 "Zebulun shall dwell by the haven of the sea; He shall become a haven for ships, and his border shall adjoin Sidon.

Zebulun, whose name means habitation, is the tenth son of Jacob. Of the sons of Jacob, Zebulun is one of the least popular and yet has great significance, particularly within the covenant community. In Genesis 49 we see that Zebulun metaphorically speaks of a haven, a habitation of rest from the storm. His assignment then is to be a source of comfort for those who have had to deal with tempestuous storms. This then should be the assignment of every covenant community, to be a place of comfort for all people that they may enter into the rest of God. The praises of the saints has been said to be what God inhabits. As we come into true unity, we are able to house God, thereby being equipped with the power to touch and change the lives of those that the storms of life drive our way.

Having wonderful church services is great, but the ability to touch lives is a gift of love that every covenant community should strive for. While just getting more people to fill seats is the common practice, the community practice ought to be to transform the lives of those in the seats, whether full or not. When this begins to happen, word will get out and the seats will fill.

We must remember that our job as apostles, prophets and so forth is to equip the saints to fulfill their ministries. The covenant community is broadened as we equip the saints to move beyond the confines of the facility where the church gathers. In this hour, there is a tremendous release of marketplace ministry. While some are afraid of this release, we must remain aware that Jesus was the great carpenter who never built a church made of wood. Interestingly, Jesus talked about the Kingdom more than seventy-five times while only speaking of the church twice. Whether we want to accept it or not, the saints are beginning to understand that they have been released on the earth by God to fulfill purposes beyond "going to church". As opposed to entrapping the saints, we should release them as they mature with the understanding that they are to remain in covenant that the community may broaden in its effectiveness.

CHAPTER 4

Beware of the Cripplers

Jude 8-11, NKJV

8 Likewise also these dreamers defile the flesh, reject authority, and speak evil of dignitaries. 9 Yet Michael the archangel, in contending with the devil, when he disputed about the body of Moses, dared not bring against him a reviling accusation, but said, "The Lord rebuke you!" 10 But these speak evil of whatever they do not know; and whatever they know naturally, like brute beasts, in these things they corrupt themselves. 11 Woe to them! For they have gone in the way of Cain, have run greedily in the error of Balaam for profit, and perished in the rebellion of Korah.

While there are those who do not believe that a child of God can be demon possessed, an individual can become subject to demonic influences due to ignorance and lack of transformation. As local covenant communities are being established and brought into order, it is very crucial that we understand that there are cripplers and assassins that seek to bring down the purposes of God. While we are not alarmed by the onslaught, we must be aware of potential problems with the understanding that there is no weapon that can form against a true covenant community and prosper. Three such cripplers that we must be aware of are listed in the book of Jude in verse 11: the Cain, Balaam and Korah spirits which have the potential to be loosed among us as well as other spirits such as the Absalom and Jezebel spirits. Tons of literature is available on the Jezebel spirit so I will not focus much on that spirit other than to say that Jezebel is not a "woman thing". This spirit is of the feminine gene because she reproduces and defiles everything that she touches. We must do all that we can to stop these malicious spirits from overtaking the people of God and ultimately defiling the community. While I am certainly not jumping on the bandwagon with those who live in the Church with a constant defensive warring attitude, I do want to make us aware of the subtlety that if ignored could be dangerous. Let's take a look at the Cain spirit first.

Genesis 4:1-15, NKJV

*1 Now Adam knew Eve his wife, and she conceived and bore Cain, and said, "I have acquired a man from the LORD." 2 Then she bore again, this time his brother Abel. Now Abel was a keeper of sheep, but Cain was a tiller of the ground. 3 And in the process of time it came to pass that Cain brought an offering of the fruit of the ground to the LORD. 4 Abel also brought of the firstborn of his flock and of their fat. And the LORD respected Abel and his offering, 5 but He did not respect Cain and his offering. And Cain was **very angry, and his countenance fell.** 6 So the LORD said to Cain, "Why are you angry? And why has your countenance fallen? 7 If you do well, will you not be accepted? And if you do not do well, sin lies at the door. And its desire is for you, but you should rule over it." 8 Now Cain **talked** with Abel his brother; and it came to pass, when they were in the field, that **Cain rose up against Abel his brother and killed him.** 9 Then the LORD said to Cain, "Where is Abel your brother?" He said, "I do not know. **Am I my brother's keeper?**" 10 And He said, "What have you done? The voice of your brother's blood cries out to Me from the ground. 11 So now you are **cursed from the earth**, which has opened its mouth to receive your brother's blood from your hand. 12 When you till the ground, it shall no longer yield its strength to you. A fugitive and a vagabond you shall be on the earth." 13 And Cain said to the LORD, "My punishment is greater than I can bear! 14 Surely You have driven me out this day from the face of the ground; I shall be hidden from Your face; I shall be a fugitive and a vagabond on the earth, and it will happen that anyone who finds me will kill me." 15 And the LORD said to him, "Therefore, whoever kills Cain, vengeance shall be taken on him sevenfold." And the LORD set a mark on Cain, lest anyone finding him should kill him.*

The Cain spirit brings forth competition, jealousy, and revenge. As a result of the negligence of Cain, his offering was not respected by God. The bi-product of his negligence—Cain turns against his unsuspecting brother over the response of God towards his offering. While God is not a respecter of persons, he is definitely a respecter of principles. As we will discuss further in chapter 5, the offering is always symbolic of the heart of the individual. This is why verses 4 and 5 specifically identify "Abel and his offering" and "Cain and his offering". Thus, I personally believe that we must do away with the concept of competitive giving in the church because of the disasters that it creates within the covenant community. I do not want to exhaust all of chapter 5 but I do want to mention the truth that there is a danger in attaching the blessings of God to a particular amount in giving because it opens the door to the spirit of Cain. Without being overly suspicious of every person who walks through our community doors, we must be on the lookout for people within the community who have a fallen countenance. Angry or jealous people are dangerous for a covenant community because you do not know where they will launch their attack on members of the community. Oh how Abel must have felt as he realized that his attack was the result of pleasing God. Good people die when the community is corrupt with bitter people who give God less than their best. There is no doubt that if you are a leader or pastor you are familiar with people who carry the Cain spirit. These individuals must be spotted and corrected so as to not kill innocent people who just want to please the Father. The spirit of Cain will compete for recognition in any way possible and then raise the head of jealousy against those who are not even aware that there is a competition going on. Pastor, spiritual leader, or whoever, be careful of those who are constantly competing for attention, they could be the person who kills their brothers and then act like they have no idea what you are talking about when you confront them about their action.

It is noteworthy that, contrary to popular belief, God does not curse Cain. Rather, God demonstrates himself as the informant who pronounces the curse that is upon Cain from the earth. The truth is that some actions carry their own consequences. God doesn't have to kill Cain for killing his brother, the judgment from the earth is more than enough to bring vengeful Cain to his knees. Now, he who has killed his brother is seeking mercy so as to not encounter the same spirit that he has unleashed upon his brother. God, being the merciful God that he is, provides protection for Cain even though he is guilty. It is not the person that we are after; it is the spirit that must be brought down. As we discover this sadistic spirit of competition, jealousy, and vengeance, we don't have to kill the individual in the process.

If we are not careful, the same spirit that we are out to remove from our midst, could defile us and cause us to become subject to the Cain spirit by being overreactionaries who kill people and promote this evil spirit. We, as spiritual leaders, must therefore not seek to destroy individuals who have destroyed others. Rather, we must through discernment and wisdom, identify the spirit and bring it down.

2 Corinthians 10:4-6, NKJV

*4 For the weapons of our warfare are not carnal but mighty in God for **pulling down** strongholds, 5 casting down arguments and every high thing that exalts itself against the knowledge of God, bringing every thought into captivity **to the obedience of Christ**, 6 and being ready to **punish all disobedience** when your obedience is fulfilled.*

We must begin to blow the trumpet of God amongst the people of God to bring down every high thing that exalts itself against the knowledge of God's design for the unity of the saints. Too much work goes into building a covenant community to let a Cain spirit come in and begin to reproduce itself among the faithful. As we keep covenant community before the people, the people will begin to fulfill the lifestyle which in and of itself will exterminate the Cain spirit.

While the Cain spirit is certainly a crippler in a covenant community, the Absolom spirit is equally exasperating and must be brought down as well.

2 Samuel 15:2-6, NKJV

*2 Now Absalom would rise early and stand beside the way to the gate. So it was, whenever anyone who had a lawsuit **came to the king for a decision**, that Absalom would call to him and say, "What city are you from?" And he would say, "Your servant is from such and such a tribe of Israel." 3 Then Absalom would say to him, "Look, your case is good and right; **but there is no deputy of the king to hear you**." 4 Moreover Absalom would say, **"Oh, that I were made judge in the land, and everyone who has any suit or cause would come to me; then I would give him justice**." 5 And so it was, whenever anyone came near to bow down to him, that he would put out his hand and take him and kiss him. 6 In this manner Absalom acted toward all Israel who came to the king for judgment. **So Absalom stole the hearts of the men of Israel.***

While the spirit of Cain is one who competes with those who are receiving recognition for their excellence in service, the spirit of Absalom, much like the Jezebel spirit, desires to take down leadership and establish itself as the authority. This spirit certainly should not be entertained in the least. This type of corrupt influence can spell disaster for a covenant community. This is in part because everyone within the covenant community has not necessarily arrived to maturity to recognize rebellion when it rises. Again, this must be discussed because of the subtlety of this spirit. The Absolom spirit does not immediately expose itself, but slowly releases nuggets of discontentment with leadership. This cerebral assassin is hunting for those who will succumb to the damnable influence and ultimately accept demarcation. This spirit plays on the hearts of those who are dealing with various issues within and outside of the community. Sadly, many have bowed to this subtle spirit and many churches have been split and some even destroyed because the spirit of Absalom was not handled appropriately. This spirit must be cast out! Demons can not be counseled out, they must be cast out. This spirit must be called out and the individual must be brought into full deliverance through proper teaching and application of truth. As the heart of the individual for the community is discerned by appropriate leadership, determinants are made. There are times when this individual who has given over to this spirit must be completely released from the covenant community. Again, we are not trying to kill the individual, but we can not allow a known "wolf in sheep clothing" to continue to propagate its attack against leadership.

Not only should the set ministry bring down such a diabolical force but those of the community should as well. Entertaining this spirit will cause those who silently observe to ultimately become convinced by the corrupt influencer. Thus everyone must be prepared to answer appropriately to community opposition.

Joshua 1:16-18, NKJV
16 So they answered Joshua, saying, "All that you command us we will do, and wherever you send us we will go. 17 Just as we heeded Moses in all things, so we will heed you. Only the LORD your God be with you, as He was with Moses. 18 Whoever rebels against your command and does not heed your words, in all that you command him, shall be put to death. Only be strong and of good courage."

No leader should have to spend his or her time watching their every move as to not offend someone who will ultimately decide to split the church. One way this can be handled is through more responsible and wise leadership from the set ministry gift of the house. We must not confirm grace on the lives of people too fast, for the results can be devastating for the individual and for the community as a whole. The confirmation of grace should only be released in the proper time and through much prayerful consideration.

1 Timothy 5:22 KJV
22 Lay hands suddenly on no man, neither be partaker of other men's sins: keep thyself pure.

2 Timothy 1:6, NKJV
6 Therefore I remind you to stir up the gift of God which is in you through the laying on of my hands.

As a child I remember 1 Timothy 5:22 being quoted as a person prepared to lay hands on someone who was sick or needed prayer. As I began to understand the scriptures more clearly, I learned that this sudden laying on of hands had nothing to do with praying for someone who was sick or in need of prayer, but rather the laying on of hands referred to the confirming of grace on the life of an individual. As men and women of God, we cannot afford to confirm grace on the life of an individual with haste. Everyone in leadership should be tested before they are given charge in the community of God. One of the sad indictments on many churches is that we have adopted this concept of testing through intellect only, without regard for testing "relationally". All spiritual sons and daughters of your community must be tested and retested.

This does not, however, mean that we never trust any of those who follow us. It means that we should not be so quick to place people in authority. A good rule of thumb is, if they crave leadership too quickly, don't place them. Those who typically make for good leaders are not those who have served in another house or those who are obviously gifted. Rather, the greatest leaders tend to be those who aren't excited about being in leadership. Why, you may ask, because these are the ones who recognize the awesome responsibility that goes along with leadership and tend to remain submitted as a result.

This brings us to another important crippler of covenant community, too much responsibility on one person. In the initial stages of the church, perhaps there are not many gifted people with understanding that can be placed in authority. As the community grows, the responsibility must also shift. This shifting of the weight of responsibility requires wisdom and grace. Moses realized through the wisdom of counsel from Jethro, his father-in-law, that he could not handle the weight of the responsibility of leading the children of Israel on his own.

Exodus 18:15-23, NKJV

15 And Moses said to his father-in-law, "Because the people come to me to inquire of God. 16 When they have a difficulty, they come to me, and I judge between one and another; and I make known the statutes of God and His laws." 17 So Moses' father-in-law said to him, "The thing that you do is not good. 18 Both you and these people who are with you will **surely wear yourselves out. For this thing is too much for you; you are not able to perform it by yourself.** *19 Listen now to my voice; I will give you counsel and God will be with you: Stand before God for the people, so that you may bring the difficulties to God. 20 And you shall teach them the statutes and the laws, and show them the way in which they must walk and the work they must do. 21 Moreover you shall* **select from all the people able men, such as fear God, men of truth, hating covetousness; and place such over them to be rulers of thousands, rulers of hundreds, rulers of fifties, and rulers of tens**. *22 And let them judge the people at all times. Then it will be that every great matter they shall bring to you, but every small matter they themselves shall judge. So* **it will be easier for you, for they will bear the burden with you**. *23 If you do this thing, and God so commands you, then you will be able to endure, and all this people will also go to their place in peace."*

Many church fellowships have collapsed prematurely because there was no understanding of those in leadership that the weight of ministry is to be shared and not carried on the shoulder of one man. When the children of Egypt came through the Red Sea they were led by Moses. When they passed through the Jordan they were led by the ark on the shoulders of the priests along with Joshua.

Not only should leadership be careful not to carry too much of the burden on their shoulders as we discussed in chapter 2, but the leader must also be careful not to put too much burden on the shoulders of those that they place in authority.

Exodus 18:21

21 Moreover you shall select from all the people able men, such as fear God, men of truth, hating covetousness; and place such over them to be rulers of thousands, rulers of hundreds, rulers of fifties, and rulers of tens.

Immediately, we should notice the awesome task that Moses must face. He must find men who qualify for leadership through a scope provided by Jethro. First, they must be men of ability. As the community increases in population, leadership must through a careful eye, recognize those with abilities. Ability alone, however, is not nearly suitable for measurement of one's qualification to be placed in authority. The individuals must also fear God, which is to say that they understand authority and submit to the chain of command. No one has the right to rule who does not understand that their measure of rule is limited to the degree of their submission. These men must also be men of truth. The word truth here can be likened unto sincerity in terms of having no hidden agenda. Lastly, they do not have the Cain or Absolom spirit because they hate covetousness.

As these leaders are identified, they then must be placed, based upon their abilities, to handle issues and people. Some are made captains of thousands, while others are made captains of tens. We have in verse twenty-two of the eighteenth chapter of Exodus a model for leaders to follow in placing authority. While one may possess all four qualities given by Jethro, there may be variance in the gifting of individuals as well as the level of dependability which means there must be a difference in the degree of authority released to such individuals.

All of these individuals along with intercessors (which should be everyone from the set leadership down to the youngest saint in the community) serve as gatekeepers. The gatekeepers' job was not like Absolom standing at the gate stealing the hearts of men. On the contrary, gatekeepers should be men and women who first and foremost are of one heart with the set leadership. These individuals through great discernment are able to strengthen leadership by identifying those who attempt to enter the community disguised in pseudo submission with impure motives. These gatekeepers should not focus on those who are coming in solely, but must also oversee those who are already a part of the community. Present members of the community also have the potential to be defiled from things outside of the community if not aggressively applying the life of covenant community as it is presented from leadership.

These gatekeepers must be careful not to lose the purity of keeping the gates by turning into out-of-control overreactionaries who walk in a spirit of suspicion or function in complete judgment. This type of madness will result in no one entering the covenant community because the gatekeepers have become gateclosers, who refuse to allow anyone entrance because they have a spirit of fear that everyone who is drawn to the gravitational pull of the community is coming to do harm. You may say, well let's just get rid of intercessors, gatekeepers, and the prophetic totally to stop this from happening. Woe! To do that is to rid the community of the great gifts of the prophetic and discernment. We must have a dimension of discernment to protect the integrity of the community. We don't get rid of these things, rather we continue to mature and direct those who function in this capacity. The gatekeepers, through wisdom and understanding, recognize that their job is to demonstrate love for the community and for people by identifying cripplers and make leadership aware of their presence. When leadership is aware of their presence, the gatekeeper or intercessor has fulfilled his or her job. While the gatekeeper may continue to pray against this foul spirit, leadership must be allowed to handle the situation through the wisdom of God if and when necessary.

Ephesians 4:1-3, NKJV
1 I, therefore, the prisoner of the Lord, beseech you to walk worthy of the calling with which you were called, 2 with all lowliness and gentleness, with longsuffering, bearing with one another in love, 3 endeavoring to keep the unity of the Spirit in the bond of peace.

The bond of peace is absolutely essential for the maturation of the covenant community. Peace must be exhibited and made manifest in all that we say and do. The church has been seen as trifling and manipulative, but we as a covenant community are called to present a glorious manifestation of Kingdom peace. To accomplish this awesome task, we must rid our communities of the Cain, Absolom, Jezebel and other advancement breaking spirits. When we purify the house by purifying the people in Christ, then we will see the Lord add to the house of peace. One thing is for sure, if the Lord really adds to the house, he will not add any form of discord and disunity that will paralyze otherwise mobile, advancing, covenant communities.

Proverbs 6:16-19, KJV
16 These six things doth the LORD hate: yea, seven are an abomination unto him: 17 A proud look, a lying tongue, and hands that shed innocent blood, 18 A heart that deviseth wicked imaginations, feet that be swift in running to mischief, 19 A false witness that speaketh lies, and he that soweth discord among brethren.

Absalom is a kindred spirit to Korah.

Numbers 16:1-3

Now Korah the son of Izhar, the son of Kohath, the son of Levi, with Dathan and Abiram the sons of Eliab, and On the son of Peleth, sons of Reuben, took men; 2 and they rose up before Moses with some of the children of Israel, two hundred and fifty leaders of the congregation, representatives of the congregation, men of renown. 3 They gathered together against Moses and Aaron, and said to them, "You take too much upon yourselves, for all the congregation is holy, every one of them, and the LORD is among them. Why then do you exalt yourselves above the assembly of the LORD?"

Korah, much like Absalom, is desirous of making a name for himself. Korah is more challenging than Absalom because of his powerful influence on leadership. While Absalom preyed upon poor, unsuspecting individuals who may not have been pleased with decisions made by leadership, Korah uses his influence upon individuals of rank. These men of renown, according to the scriptures, stood with Korah to challenge Moses and Aaron. The complaint was that Moses and Aaron assumed too much responsibility for the assembly. The settlement of the priesthood upon Aaron is the central means of controversy for those who have joined Korah. They felt that this honor was too much of a decision for Moses to make exclusively. The failure of Korah and the others who have risen against Moses is that Moses has not taken this responsibility upon himself; rather he was selected and set in leadership by God. Therefore, as Moses will clarify in his response to these honor aspirers, they were not merely rising up against Moses but against God himself. Great contempt is brought upon those who function with the Korah spirit, who aspire honor that they are not prepared to walk in. Set leader, do not find yourself intimidated by those who want confirmation to function in areas that they are not graced to function in. Consider this, if they will rise up against you from the present level of authority that they have, do you think that they will rise up against you if you give them more authority?

This spirit is often perpetuated by those who want the community to remain in the era of deacon or committee run churches. Often, people who have this spirit at work in their lives are those who want to have a say in every decision made by set leadership. As with the Cain and Absalom spirit, this must not be permitted nor taken lightly. The covenant community is not a democracy and can not function as such. God raises a leader and that leader is responsible for the establishment of order and the conferring of grace on the lives of those who are in submission to the vision of the house, as discussed in chapter two.

It is not by chance that Cain came against his brother Abel, Absalom came against his father David, and Korah came against his cousin Moses. While I do not want to overplay the obvious, I do feel it necessary to mention that often, some of the biggest challenges of covenant community are biological family connections. Sometimes, such individuals have to be watched carefully because they can have a heightened proclivity to get too close to leadership to the point of being common as a result of their biological kinship. Biological kinship does not necessarily mean spiritual kinship. This is often a threat to covenant community that must be handled delicately yet thoroughly. This should cause leaders not to be so quick to place authority on individuals just because they have a biological connection. If there is no spiritual connection, the biological has no place in the community, in terms of prominence.

Perhaps you have noticed that I left out one of the cripplers mentioned in the book of Jude, Balaam. I have intentionally reserved Balaam for last because this spirit, as far as I'm concerned at this point in time, is the one that not only creeps into the people but also creeps into the leadership. There are numerous examples of the manifestation of this spirit within the leadership of the church throughout the years.

In Revelation 2:14, God addresses the church in Pergamos for adopting the doctrine of Balaam. Balaam instructed Balak to "put a stumbling block before the children of Israel, to eat things sacrificed to idols and to commit sexual immorality." Balaam is noted in scripture for his inconsistency as he mixed good and evil. One moment he's blessing and another moment he's cursing. This sounds much like the leadership that we have in many circles of Christendom which is manifesting greatly in sexual immorality. We all must be careful that our lives live up to the gospel that we preach. If we declare one thing and live another, we give off an unclear sound. I certainly do not want to join the bandwagon of those who consistently bash church leadership, but at the risk of sounding familiar I do want to declare that the spirit of Balaam must be brought down in the pulpits of America and beyond. This is not a call for spiritual private investigators to terrorize all leadership to find areas of immorality. This is a call for repentance in both the pulpit and the pew.

Not only are men and women of God demonstrating inconsistencies in our declaration and our walk, but so are many of the saints. The spirit of Balaam is consistent inconsistencies. Some of the saints are dependably undependable. You can expect those who walk in the spirit of Balaam to say with their mouths how much they love the community all the while they don't give cheerfully of their treasure and are unfaithful to the ministry and to God.

Ironically, the book of Revelation calls these diabolical spirits frogs. As soon as you have these spirits identified, captured and under authority, they hop elsewhere. Beware, lest we become overreactionaries who constantly live in a defensive posture and seek to run everyone out of the church that may have some tendencies of these or other violating spirits, let's remember:

1 Corinthians 11:18b-19

. . . I hear that there are divisions among you, and in part I believe it. 19 For there must also be factions among you, that those who are approved *may* be recognized among you.

You can spend all of your time trying to put out every single problem that may exist in your ministry, or you can come to a degree of understanding whereby you comprehend that sometimes these violators may be released to distract you from recognizing those who are truly committed to the covenant community. When this is understood clearly, ministry gifts will be able to bless the house with truth that will edify the body instead of perpetuating constant bitterness within the community as a result of poor ministry that is preoccupied with just trying to keep fires down. The declaration of truth will often rid the community of many of the problem starters. If they can walk away from you, you are probably better off without them!

1 John 2:19

19 They went out from us, but they were not of us; for if they had been of us, they would have continued with us; but they went out that they might be made manifest, that none of them were of us.

Don't spend your time trying to make people fit where they do not belong. Even if they remain in the congregation, you must pronounce like Jesus that you know all those who are yours. Your what? Your bone!

Ezekiel 37:11-14, 21-22 NKJV

11 Then He said to me, "Son of man, these bones are the whole house of Israel. They indeed say, 'Our bones are dry, our hope is lost, and we ourselves are cut off!' 12 Therefore prophesy and say to them, 'Thus says the Lord GOD: "Behold, O My people, I will open your graves and cause you to come up from your graves, and bring you into the land of Israel. 13 Then you shall know that I am the LORD, when I have opened your graves, O My people, and brought you up from your graves. 14 I will put My Spirit in you, and you shall live, and I will place you in your own land. Then you shall know that I, the LORD, have spoken it and performed it," says the LORD.'

21 "Then say to them, 'Thus says the Lord GOD: "Surely I will take the children of Israel from among the nations, wherever they have gone, and will gather them from every side and bring them into their own land; 22 and I will make them one nation in the land, on the mountains of Israel; and one king shall be king over them all; they shall no longer be two nations, nor shall they ever be divided into two kingdoms again.

As leaders of covenant communities, we must perceive that all who come through the doors of our ministry are not called to continue perpetually with us. If the ministry is vibrant and attractive, people will join. This however does not necessarily mean that they are permanently planted within the ministry. Therefore, we must remain open to the fact that saints of God will continue to realign from one ministry to another until they hear the voice of God and know where they are to be aligned. As a pastor in the city of Fort Worth, I am thoroughly convinced that I am not locally aligned with every citizen of our city. As a result, I am not surprised when members come and go. While I certainly make every attempt to make our entire constituency feel welcomed and loved, I am fully aware that everyone is not called to be with me. This mindset relieves the set ministry of the stress of trying to hold on to everyone who finds the ministry attractive for the moment.

1 John 2:19, NKJV

19 They went out from us, but they were not of us; for if they had been of us, they would have continued with us; but they went out that they might be made manifest, that none of them were of us.

CHAPTER 5

Cost of Advancement

The Antioch church is the model apostolic church in the book of Acts. It was from Antioch that the team of Barnabas and Paul as well as Paul and Silas were sent out to do apostolic works. It is highly imperative that each covenant community recognizes that the house is not just designed to bless those who are a part of that particular fellowship. Every house must be a house with a mission. This mission must be identified and proclaimed as new shifts in the spirit are released prophetically. The prophetic or proceeding word that releases presence and purpose must supercede the preaching of possessions. Not to accomplish this is for the prophet of the house, or set ministry, to keep the saints infantile and impotent. We as covenant communities must function with a mandate to break the powers of darkness by simply dispelling them through the power of the light of God's truth.

Worship and intercession precede the prophetic word of truth and transfer the people from the earthly realm to the realm of the spirit. Because God lives in glory, we must create an atmosphere of glory on the earth that is conducive to his presence which will ultimately release the miraculous and bring us further into shared glory with the Father. When we gather, there must be an understanding that worship and intercession are our divine assignments whereby an atmosphere of glory is created in which God is able to speak without limitation and reform us into his image.

It is noteworthy of the Antioch church (the sending church, the apostolic house, the covenant community) that although Barnabus mentors Paul, the Apostle Paul accomplishes more in our Bible. The reason is because the son is supposed to supercede the father as spiritual impartation takes place. As set ministry within a covenant community, each time we mount the podium, whether to preach or otherwise, there should be a transfer that takes place like no other speaker can give. True sons and daughters are not in place to move up the ecclesiastic ladder, rather they are in place to submit to headship while ministering to the needs of headship as they receive impartation. When this principle is followed, there is a flow of power and grace that supercedes the anointing and gifting of any one individual. This is the principal of legal spiritual withdrawal.

Psalm 86:16

16 O turn unto me, and have mercy upon me; give thy strength unto thy servant, and save the son of thine handmaid.

2 Kings 2:9

9 And so it was, when they had crossed over, that Elijah said to Elisha, "Ask! What may I do for you, before I am taken away from you?" Elisha said, "Please let a double portion of your spirit be upon me."

While many are after the mantle of set ministry gifts or spiritual fathers, there must be an understanding of what I call legal spiritual withdrawal. I believe that just as individuals must make a deposit in the bank before a withdrawal transaction can take place, the same is true of those who are desirous to see a manifestation of the mantle of their covering operate in their lives. The servant of Psalm 86 can only request the strength of the one he serves after demonstrating the commitment of a true servant. Elisha can only receive the double portion of Elijah after passing the tremendous commitment exam of seeing Elijah eye to eye when he is taken away.

What is the necessary deposit for legal spiritual withdrawal? There must be a manifestation of relationship which involves one's time, talent, and treasure. In this chapter, I will focus much of our energy on the power of the treasure. Before I do, we must look, however briefly at time and talent. While we are in a fast paced society, where everything is done in a hurry-up offense style of living, it is important that we understand that time is one of the most important commodities of our day.

Ephesians 5:15-16, NKJV

15 See then that you walk circumspectly, not as fools but as wise, 16 redeeming the time, because the days are evil.

In the covenant community where I serve, the people of God understand that there are some things that I am willing to waste, but my time is certainly not one of them. For those that I mentor, cover spiritually, counsel, or advise, I always begin the relationship by making it clear that my time cannot be wasted at all. If legal spiritual withdrawal is to take place, people must be taught that they must be willing to wisely use their time applying to their lives the wisdom keys that have been released within the community. The challenge then becomes one by which we must determine whether we are gathering for the purpose of gathering or if there is a glorious outcome attached to our gatherings. When this is clear, true sons of God are not challenged to give of their time. When transformation is a bi-product, time is not wasted but invested.

While time is a necessary deposit, one's talents must also be submitted to the set ministry of the house. One of the saddest moments of a house is when someone is placed in leadership or whatever form of ministry prematurely. It is my conviction that everyone who comes into Hope of Glory that I do not know intimately comes in and submits their gift to the house before it can be used. Often, gifted and talented people can be the biggest nightmare for a ministry. Man or woman of God, test the character and discipline of every individual who comes into your setting with a gift or talent before you put them in the high seat. You can avoid utter embarrassment later. If Judas is going to be in the house, put him on the volunteer committee before you put him on your payroll.

To avoid humiliation and regret later, we must test a person's heart not only for God but for the ministry before we make them prominent in the community. Submission of one's talent enables the person to demonstrate that he or she has no ulterior motive. No matter how gifted or talented an individual is, he or she has no right to minister if they are unable to submit their gift to the house. Microphone hungry people tend to lack the discipline necessary to edify the house. The gift or talent must be submitted to leadership until such time as leadership deems that the gift or talent can edify the house.

Now that we have discussed in part, time and talent, we now want to focus on the divine nature of covenant as it is exhibited in terms of one's treasures. It is important to understand that the abundance of your giving demonstrates the degree of your covenant and it is directly proportionate to the functionality of ministry.

Romans 10:15, KJV

15 And how shall they preach, except they be sent? as it is written, How beautiful are the feet of them that preach the gospel of peace, and bring glad tidings of good things!

This text has often been seen from the single perspective of being sent by God. I certainly do not want to diminish this truth. I do however want to broaden our scope to perceive the duality of the sending. We have understood for years that there can be no message without an original messenger. Some have gone as far as to adopt the concept that the preacher is nothing more than the mail man who comes to deliver the mail and makes statements such as, "don't get mad at me, I am just the mail man." While I understand what the preacher means by this statement, I am not sure that it is wise to see the preacher as merely a mail man. First of all, the preacher is sent with a clear message. I don't know about you but I would not be too excited if my mailman broke the seal of my mail and knew the content of the message before me. Furthermore, I do not have an intimate relationship with my mail man, while I appreciate the care that he takes in delivering mail. Thus, the sent preacher is significantly more than a mailman. The sent preacher is sent with a mandate and a responsibility to shine forth the light of God's glorious truth to dispel darkness and ignorance for those who will adhere to the message.

The sending of Romans 10:15 goes beyond being sent by God. The model church that we have chosen for our consideration in this chapter is the Antioch church. This church was in fact a sending church. If the church of God is going to reach the masses and bring forth revelation and truth, we must not lock all of our men and women of God within the four walls of our local community building. Therefore, the sending must also happen through the release of our treasures into the house.

Matthew 2:11

11 And when they had come into the house, they saw the young Child with Mary His mother, and fell down and worshiped Him. And when they had opened their treasures, they presented gifts to Him: gold, frankincense, and myrrh.

If you remember, we looked at the corporate man as the body of Christ back in chapter three. I believe that this truth can be applied here in Matthew 2. What makes an individual wise is when he can bring his worship and his treasures into the community. Many want to come to the gathering to worship but not many are willing to open their treasures and present them before the Lord as well. I remember sitting in a church setting when someone said that George Washington was definitely going to heaven because he always comes to church! If George is the most faithful member of your covenant community, there is a great possibility that you do not have the hearts of those who are a part of your community.

Matthew 6:21

21 For where your treasure is, there your heart will be also.

Galatians 6:6-7, NKJV

6 Let him who is taught the word share in all good things with him who teaches. 7 Do not be deceived, God is not mocked; for whatever a man sows, that he will also reap.

---

1 Corinthians 9:7-11, NIV

7 Who serves as a soldier at his own expense? Who plants a vineyard and does not eat of its grapes? Who tends a flock and does not drink of the milk? 8 Do I say this merely from a human point of view? Doesn't the Law say the same thing? 9 For it is written in the Law of Moses: "Do not muzzle an ox while it is treading out the grain." Is it about oxen that God is concerned? 10 Surely he says this for us, doesn't he? Yes, this was written for us, because when the plowman plows and the thresher threshes, they ought to do so in the hope of sharing in the harvest. 11 If we have sown spiritual seed among you, is it too much if we reap a material harvest from you?

The earth's water cycle is made up of four main parts: evaporation, condensation, precipitation, and collection. While I do not want to give an exhaustive explanation of the water cycle, I do believe that an inquisitive glance can help to foster our understanding of the principle of reciprocity. The earth has a limited amount of water; therefore, the earth has to cycle water through a system of reciprocity. The sun evaporates water from the collection (bodies of water) and then the clouds send forth water unto the land through precipitation (raining). If the bodies of water do not send water up in the form of vapor there can be no downpour of water in the form of rain. Could this be the revelation that the Apostle Paul is conveying to both the church of Galatia and the church of Corinth? When there is no flow going up into headship, there can be no, or at least a limited amount of, flow coming down to the collection—the community. We must develop a complete understanding in the covenant community that we as a body are responsible to do our part in the duality of sending men and women of God that revelation may continue to flow in purity and potency. While I am not at all saying that the man of God should bleed the house of God, I am saying that the community must not allow the man of God to labor and not pour back into him that he may continue to go forth in the strength of God. Again I say, the abundance, or lack thereof, of your giving demonstrates the degree of your covenant and it is directly proportionate to the functionality of ministry.

2 Corinthians 9:6-15

*6 But this I say: He who sows sparingly will also reap sparingly, and he who sows bountifully will also reap bountifully. 7 So let each one give as he purposes in his heart, not grudgingly or of necessity; for God loves a cheerful giver. 8 And God is able to make all grace abound toward you, that you, always having all sufficiency in all things, may have **an abundance for every good work**. 9 As it is written: "He has dispersed abroad, He has given to the poor; His righteousness endures forever." 10 Now may He who supplies seed to the sower, and bread for food, supply and multiply the seed you have sown and **increase the fruits of your righteousness**, 11 while you* *are enriched in **everything for all liberality, which causes thanksgiving through us to God**. 12 For the administration of this service not only supplies the needs of the saints, but also is abounding through many thanksgivings to God, 13 while, through the proof of this ministry, they glorify God for the obedience of your confession to the gospel of Christ, and for your liberal sharing with them and all men, 14 and by their prayer for you, who long for you because of the exceeding grace of God in you. 15 Thanks be to God for His indescribable gift!*

The mentality of sowing in the covenant community to reap personal benefits of material wealth must be brought into wholeness. I am not one who believes that God wants us to be poor and that any form of material wealth is of the devil. However, it seems that there needs to be a serious realignment in the church as it pertains to the Kingdom purpose and assignment of monetary prosperity. We must financially support true ministry. It is important to understand that the abundance of your giving demonstrates the degree of your covenant and it is directly proportionate to the functionality of ministry. The real increase that comes through funding true ministry is the release of the grace of God within you. The promise of this text is not financial prosperity but a multiplication of the seed that the fruit of righteousness may ever increase.

Malachi 3:8-12 NKJV
8 "Will a man rob God? Yet you have robbed Me! But you say, 'In what way have we robbed You?' In tithes and offerings.

Robbed is defined to cause bodily harm for the purpose of taking the possession of another. The withholding of the treasure in this text is literally the weapon used for the robbery. What do you take? Not the tithe and the offering. What you take is the life that is supposed to be released from the house and given to others through the covenant community.

*9 You are cursed with a curse, For you have robbed Me, Even this whole nation. {**Me is the nation, the nation is me!**} 10 Bring all the tithes **into** the storehouse, That there may be **meat** in My house, And try Me now in this," Says the LORD of hosts, "If I will not **open you** the windows of heaven And **pour you out** such blessing That there will not be room enough to receive it.*

Those who do not faithfully release finances liberally and cheerfully at best receive the milk of the word but not the meat of the word which transforms your life and causes you to demonstrate the Kingdom of God. Only those who release finances into the storehouse, store up revelation that can be drawn upon at any given point when needed. Somehow, there are a few people who have jumped on a ridiculous bandwagon who feel that the treasure should not be brought into the storehouse and left there, but that they should use their treasure to purchase things for or from the covenant community. Child of God, buying things for the church is a wonderful gesture as well as purchasing tapes and cds; however this should never be done at the neglect of bringing the treasure into the house. As we do this, God does not pour a bunch of stuff out of windows but rather God wants to open us and then pour us out to the point that the world cannot contain all that God is doing in and through our community.

11 "And I will rebuke the devourer for your sakes, So that he will not destroy the fruit of your ground, Nor shall the vine fail to bear fruit for you in the field," Says the LORD of hosts.

The devourer in this case is not the devil exclusively. While we certainly recognized that he is the ultimate devourer, this text gives room to recognize that the devourer in this case is the one who is withholding the treasure and the offering. Therefore, you cannot afford not to release hilariously your treasure while believing a seducing spirit that says you can't afford to give unto the Kingdom of God. The devourer is rebuked by God so that the covenant community does not fail to bear fruit, which we define from 2 Corinthians 9 to mean productivity. Therefore, the treasure is not just for the community but it is also necessary to keep the individual from lacking in areas that produce destiny. When we understand that our community is a part of the overall nation, we begin to understand that the effectiveness of our treasures blesses beyond our local community.

*12 And all nations **will call you blessed**, For you will be a **delightful land**," Says the LORD of hosts.*

While the saints should not be brow-beaten concerning tithes and offerings, there should reside a great love for the ministry that prompts us to give so that our community and beyond is a land of delight and not struggle. The release of the treasures of those who are a part of the covenant community, as well as set ministries, who should be submitted to spiritual fathers, causes increases in the advancement of the agenda of the Kingdom of God. We need an open heaven in this hour like never before. Obedience to this principle of releasing our treasures to the Kingdom before the malls or this world's system is a key that will unlock heaven.

Leviticus 26:19-22, NKJV
*19 I will break the pride of your power; I will make your **heavens like iron** and your earth like bronze. 20 And your strength shall be spent in vain; for your land shall not yield its produce, nor shall the trees of the land yield their fruit. 21 'Then, if*

you walk contrary to Me, and are not willing to obey Me, I will bring on you seven times more plagues, according to your sins. 22 I will also send wild beasts among you, which shall rob you of your children, destroy your livestock, and make you few in number; and your highways shall be desolate.

We must admit that while things are exceptionally well for many, there are so many others who are in desperate need for a release of a heavenly invasion. We must send forth men and women of God through the release of our treasures that they may boldly declare open heavens.

Haggai 1:2-11, NKJV

*2 "Thus speaks the LORD of hosts, saying: 'This people say, "The time has not come, the time that the LORD's house should be built."'" 3 Then the word of the LORD came by Haggai the prophet, saying, 4 "Is it time for you yourselves to dwell in your paneled houses, and this temple to lie in ruins?" 5 Now therefore, thus says the LORD of hosts:" Consider your ways! 6 "You have sown much, and bring in little; You eat, but do not have enough; You drink, but you are not filled with drink; You clothe yourselves, but no one is warm; And he who earns wages, Earns wages to put into a bag with holes." 7 Thus says the LORD of hosts: "Consider your ways! 8 Go up to the mountains and bring wood and build the temple, that I may take pleasure in it and be glorified," says the LORD. 9 "You looked for much, but indeed it came to little; and when you brought it home, I blew it away. Why?" says the LORD of hosts. "Because of My house that is in ruins, while every one of you runs to his own house. 10 **Therefore the heavens above you withhold the dew**, and the earth withholds its fruit. 11 For I called for a drought on the land and the mountains, on the grain and the new wine and the oil, on whatever the ground brings forth, on men and livestock, and on all the labor of your hands."*

If this sounds like your covenant community, keep reading to get the key to an open heaven!

Haggai 2:6-9, 18-22

*6 "For thus says the LORD of hosts: 'Once more (it is a little while) **I will shake heaven and earth**, the sea and dry land; 7 and I will shake all nations, and they shall come to the Desire of All Nations, and I will fill this temple with glory,' says the LORD of hosts. 8 'The silver is Mine, and the gold is Mine,' says the LORD of hosts. 9 'The glory of this latter temple shall be greater than the former,' says the LORD of hosts. 'And in this place I will give peace,' says the LORD of hosts."*

*18 'Consider now from this day forward, from the twenty-fourth day of the ninth month, **from the day that the foundation of the LORD's temple was laid—consider it**: 19 Is the seed still in the barn? As yet the vine, the fig tree, the pomegranate, and* *the olive tree have not yielded fruit. But from this day I will bless you."' 20 And again the word of the LORD came to Haggai on the twenty-fourth day of the month, saying, 21 "Speak to Zerubbabel, governor of Judah, saying:* **'I will shake heaven and earth.** *22 I will overthrow the throne of kingdoms; I will destroy the strength of the Gentile kingdoms I will overthrow the chariots and those who ride in them; The horses and their riders shall come down, Every one by the sword of his brother.*

Through the revitalization of kingdom money, the community is ignited with revelation and truth that will open new seasons for the people of God. Your season is supposed to be contagious. As the parishioners of the covenant community begin functioning appropriately with their treasures, the kingdoms of this world will be overthrown. As the community begins flowing in favor and influence, don't stop the flow of blessing with your friend who goes to another church getting mediocre word. There are many outside of the four walls of the church building who are not receiving any revealed truth, yet they are waiting in their spirit for someone to break through the door of their soul that they may also manifest what lies within them.

Jesus taught us to pray, thy kingdom come! As the Kingdom of God is made manifest in the earth through the power of a true assembly of earth and heaven, we will see an unprecedented release of kings and priests functioning together as one. This is clearly seen through the Lord Jesus Christ. On the one hand is declared to be king of kings while on the other hand he is heralded as a priest after the order of Melchizedek. Melchizedek likewise points to the manifestation of the king-priest. Priests minister in the realm of spirit through worship and intercession. Through the years the priestly anointing has been quite prevalent in the church. However, as marketplace ministry and greater understanding is evolving, we are beginning to see the kingly anointing rise from obscurity. No longer will we settle for mere praise and worship settings that lead to a good time but a poverty lifestyle. As kings, we are advancing in wealth, authority, influence, and wisdom as we continue to praise our great King of kings.

Chapter 6

The Table of Common Union

1 Corinthians 11:17-32 NKJV

17 Now in giving these instructions I do not praise you, since you come together not for the better but for the worse. 18 For first of all, when you come together as a church, I hear that there are divisions among you, and in part I believe it. 19 For there must also be factions among you, that those who are approved may be recognized among you. 20 Therefore when you come together in one place, it is not to eat the Lord's Supper. 21 For in eating, each one takes his own supper ahead of others; and one is hungry and another is drunk. 22 What! Do you not have houses to eat and drink in? Or do you despise the church of God and shame those who have nothing? What shall I say to you? Shall I praise you in this? I do not praise you. 23 For I received from the Lord that which I also delivered to you: that the Lord Jesus on the same night in which He was betrayed took bread; 24 and when He had given thanks, He broke it and said, "Take, eat; this is My body which is broken for you; do this in remembrance of Me." 25 In the same manner He also took the cup after supper, saying, "This cup is the new covenant in My blood. This do, as often as you drink it, in remembrance of Me." 26 For as often as you eat this bread and drink this cup, you proclaim the Lord's death till He comes. 27 Therefore whoever eats this bread or drinks this cup of the Lord in an unworthy manner will be guilty of the body and blood of the Lord. 28 But let a man examine himself, and so let him eat of the bread and drink of the cup. 29 For he who eats and drinks in an unworthy manner eats and drinks judgment to himself, not discerning the Lord's body. 30 For this reason many are weak and sick among you, and many sleep. 31 For if we would judge ourselves, we would not be judged. 32 But when we are judged, we are chastened by the Lord, that we may not be condemned with the world.

There are many doctrinal viewpoints of the celebration of the Eucharist, or what is more popularly known amongst Protestants as communion. However, for the sake of our discussion we will partially utilize the understanding given through John Calvin. Calvin's viewpoint of the Eucharist was that there is a strong and real spiritual presence of Christ amongst the covenant community in the person of Holy Spirit. This presence of Christ, according to Calvin, bestows grace that seals the covenant community. His understanding was that this coming together of the covenant community was a reflective view of Jesus' extreme suffering in death, coupled with a strong anticipation of the heavenly life {on the earth} that yet awaits us.

As we celebrate the Eucharist, we must constantly remind ourselves of the cost of the shed blood of Christ on His cross. I often remind the covenant community at Hope of Glory that we do not merely reflect on his sufferings but that we must also actively participate in His sufferings. This is accomplished as individuals of a covenant community die to their own agendas and wills when necessary that we may corporately live in His will. We also perceive this time of sharing as a time of fellowship and celebration of our life in Christ. As a result of coming into this place of understanding we are able to experience the "presence" that John Calvin refers to.

Philippians 3:10, NKJV
That I may know Him and the power of His resurrection, and the fellowship of His sufferings, being conformed to His death.

The Hebrew word for fellowship in Philippians 3:10 is the word koinonia, "communion, fellowship, sharing in common". The root word for koinonia is koinos, "common", translated "communion" in 1 Corinthians 10:16. To help foster our understanding we will use the symbol of the cross of Christ, which is both vertical and horizontal. Thus, it not only brings us into vertical fellowship with God but also horizontally it brings us into fellowship with those who are a part of the global body of Christ. With this foundational understanding, perhaps now we can extract from the scriptures truth for our establishment.

1 Corinthians 11:28-29, NKJV
28 But let a man examine himself, and so let him eat of the bread and drink of the cup. 29 For he who eats and drinks in an unworthy manner eats and drinks judgment to himself, not discerning the Lord's body.

There are two forms of the word examine that I would like for us to consider; dokimazo, "to prove, test, approve" and anakrino, "to examine or investigate."

Both of these words are translated, in the verb tense, examine. Interestingly, the word anakrino is also translated, "to discern."

The Apostle Paul says that a man is to examine himself. Most of the time we read the eleventh chapter of First Corinthians from an individualistic view because the Apostle is giving instructions on how an individual is to approach communion. Due to the very nature of this book, I would like for us to consider even the instructions given by the Apostle from a community perspective. To do this, we must take a closer look at "the man" who is to examine himself.

Ephesians 4:13, NKJV
*Till **we all** come to the unity of the faith and of the knowledge of the Son of God, to **a perfect man**, to the measure of the stature of the fullness of Christ.*

The message of the Apostle Paul is clear, we as individuals are supposed to become, through common union, a perfect man. We will explore this subject in another chapter with more emphasis. For now, we need to understand that if we are to experience the full "seal" of the presence of Christ during the celebration of Eucharist, the community must become a man who examines himself. This man is not just a unit but in Ephesians this man is a perfect man, or better yet, the perfect man. A perfect man cannot be a slow, sick, and sleepy one.

1 Corinthians 11:30
For this reason many are weak and sick among you, and many sleep.

Why are there many slow, sick, and sleepy people in our pews? Because we have yet to become a discerning covenant community; this releases the perfect one in and through us.

1 Corinthians 11:29
29 For he who eats and drinks in an unworthy manner eats and drinks judgment to himself, not discerning the Lord's body.

Remember, we are looking at "he" as the covenant community. A covenant community that is not discerning the Lord's body is one who should not be at the common union table. The Hebrew word for discerning here is diakrino, which shares a root with anakrino. We are to discern the Lord's body.

1 Corinthians 10:17, NKJV
*For **we**, though many, are **one bread and one body**; for we all partake of that one bread.*

—

1 Corinthians 12:27, NKJV
*Now **you are** the body of Christ, and members individually.*

If there is no sense of covenant community, then our gathering at the common union table is nothing more than a religious tradition that produces nothing more than judgment. What is the judgment? The judgment that comes is a continued state of division, which manifests itself through more slow, sick, and sleepy saints.

On the contrary however, when there is a true understanding of covenant community, there is a manifestation of synergy. Synergy comes from the Greek word sunergia, which is energy released through two or more working together. Again, "the whole is greater than the sum of its parts."

Notice in 1 Corinthians 10:17, the Apostle Paul says that we are "one bread". To understand this fully we will need to go back to the schoolmaster, the Old Testament.

Leviticus 24:5-8, NKJV
5 "And you shall take fine flour and bake twelve cakes with it. Two-tenths of an ephah shall be in each cake. 6 You shall set them in two rows, six in a row, on the pure gold table before the LORD. 7 And you shall put pure frankincense on each row, that it may be on the bread for a memorial, an offering made by fire to the LORD. 8 Every Sabbath he shall set it in order before the LORD continually, being taken from the children of Israel by an everlasting covenant."

Without getting into a complete discourse on the various spiritual understandings that we are to presently receive from the Old Testament tabernacle, it is necessary that we understand that Moses was instructed by God to build the tabernacle according to the pattern that he was shown. The tabernacle as we know it was made three dimensional. There are tremendous books in which multiple examples of three dimensional things are laid out for you. (See *The House That God Built* by Dr. Mark Hanby and *Prevail: A handbook for the Overcomer* by Dr. Kelley Varner.) For the sake of this writing, we need to understand that the Outer Court speaks of the world, while the Inner Court and Most Holy Place speak of the church and the Kingdom, respectfully.

Interestingly enough, the table of showbread is within the Inner Court along with the Candlesticks and the Altar of Incense. All three of these items play a tremendous role in church fellowship. The Candlesticks symbolize the prophetic or proceeding word of God as well as the church in the book of Revelation.

Psalm 119:105, NKJV
Your word is a lamp to my feet and a light to my path.

It is in church fellowship that we are supposed to receive revelation and illumination, which brings us inspiration and through violent application fosters our transformation. The church building was never intended to be a place where we go for the sake of meeting some religious obligation. Notice that the Altar of Incense is also found in the Inner Court, the church dimension. The Altar of Incense represents prayer and worship.

Revelation 5:8-10, NKJV

5 Now when He had taken the scroll, the four living creatures and the twenty-four elders fell down before the Lamb, each having a harp, and golden bowls full of incense, which are the prayers of the saints. 9 And they sang a new song, saying: "You are worthy to take the scroll and to open its seals; For You were slain, and have redeemed us to God by Your blood out of every tribe and tongue and people and nation, 10 And have made us kings and priests to our God; and we shall reign on the earth."

Psalm 141:2, NKJV

2 Let my prayer be set before You as incense, the lifting up of my hands as the evening sacrifice.

Most church fellowships specialize in the word, prayer and/or worship. Yet if we are going to get the fullness of this dimension and then process behind the veil into the Kingdom realm, we must embrace the table of showbread. Notice in Leviticus 24 that the bread was to be set in order on the table every Sabbath in two rows of six. Of course, we understand that the total number of cakes is 12, which is the result of taking one cake from each tribe. However, if we look at the way the table was setup we may find an interesting point. Why not set the table with five in one row and seven in another or three rows of four? To answer this seemingly insignificant question, we will need to look at biblical numerology very briefly. Two is the number of covenant which can be seen in Adam and Eve, Ruth and Naomi, God and Abraham, David and Jonathan, etc. Furthermore, six is the number of man because it was on the sixth day that God created man. Why two rows of six?—Because this table represents covenant community. When we come into the fullness of this understanding of covenant community, we cease to be two rows of six breads, and we mature to become "one bread".

Perhaps we can now come to the place where we truly discern the Lord's body so that we not have any sick among us. Let's not settle anymore for mere healing lines and healing services, let's passionately pursue covenant communities within our local assemblies to release a spirit of life whereby we walk in divine health. So that if someone should get sick, we have an immediate remedy for the situation to call for the mature of the church so that prayer may be offered up to dispel a temporary visitation from sickness. After all, wherever covenant community goes, life flows. Now, no one has time to be slow, sick, and sleepy because they are too busy living and releasing life everywhere they go. The covenant community is a tree of life in Revelation 22, wears a crown of life in James 1, has the word of life in Philippians 2, and flows as the river of life in Revelation 22.

John 10:10, NKJV

The thief does not come except to steal, and to kill, and to destroy. I have come that they may have life, and that they may have it more abundantly.

CHAPTER 7

The High Priest Only

Ephesians 2:19-22
19 Now, therefore, you are no longer strangers and foreigners, but fellow citizens with the saints and members of the household of God, 20 having been built on the foundation of the apostles and prophets, Jesus Christ Himself being the chief cornerstone, 21 in whom the whole building, being fitted together, grows into a holy temple in the Lord, 22 in whom you also are being built together for a dwelling place of God in the Spirit.

The book of Ephesians is a tremendous illustration of the covenant community. In chapter one, we are a family. Chapter two calls us a temple. Chapter three denotes a church. In chapter four we are the body, which we will explore in more detail in this chapter. Chapter five depicts a bride. And chapter six closes Ephesians with an army. Through the multiple illustrations used by the Apostle Paul, we can gleam a clear comprehension of the nature of the covenant community. This theme of the Apostle Paul is not just presented to the Church at Ephesus but to the powerful, yet dysfunctional Church at Corinth as well.

1 Corinthians 3:9
9 For we are God's fellow workers; you are God's field, you are God's building.

2 Corinthians 6:16
16 And what agreement has the temple of God with idols? For you are the temple of the living God. As God has said: "I will dwell in them and walk among them. I will be their God, and they shall be My people."

To the Church at Corinth, the Apostle depicts the covenant community as a field, building, and temple. None of these physical constructs used by the Apostle Paul can be fully functional without all of the necessary compartments fulfilling their responsibility. A temple cannot stand without a proper foundation. A building must have brick and mortar, as well as windows, carpet, wood, etc. A field must have soil, grass, fertilizer and proper water to be beautiful and green. Every one of these relies on more than one item to function. As is the case of the covenant community, in order to function properly, we need one another.

We are built on a solid foundation. Apostles, prophets, with Christ, the chief cornerstone, provide a solid foundation upon which to stand. This is why there is such demand to understand the roles of apostles and prophets in today's church. For far too long have these ascension gifts gone unnoticed or perhaps even oversimplified by those who are merely title hungry and do not have the grace to function in these areas of ministry.

While having a solid foundation is crucial for any ministry that is developing, buying land or carrying out vision, we must perceive that the building must be fitly joined together as well. While not referenced earlier, the Apostle Paul refers to himself in verse 10 of 1 Corinthians 3 as a wise master builder. As men and women of God, it is crucial that we not just place people in ministry but see to the particular place where they fit. Many will attempt to fulfill the responsibility of headship by merely putting people anywhere, in terms of leadership just to give them something to do. This is not wise building. As we seek God as to where to place individuals within the community, then and only then will the community grow up into a holy temple as a dwelling place for our God. As each brick, window, electrical outlet, etc. has a specific place of functioning, so does the body of Christ. Not only does each part of the body have its own area of functioning, but it is also dependent on the rest of the body so that the body is fully functional. Many are so driven for a big house that they fail to comprehend that you should never compromise health for size. A good set ministry gift understands that you have to build a church before you build a building.

1 Corinthians 12:12-23

12 For as the body is one and has many members, but all the members of that one body, being many, are one body, so also is Christ. 13 For by one Spirit we were all baptized into one body—whether Jews or Greeks, whether slaves or free—and have all been made to drink into one Spirit. 14 For in fact the body is not one member but many. 15 If the foot should say, "Because I am not a hand, I am not of the body," is it therefore not of the body? 16 And if the ear should say, "Because I am not an eye, I am not of the body," is it therefore not of the body? 17 If the whole body were an eye, where would be the hearing? If the whole were hearing, where would be the smelling? 18 But now God has set the members, each one of them, in the body just as He pleased. 19 And if they were all one member, where would the body be? 20 But now indeed there are many members, yet one body. 21 And the eye cannot say to the hand, "I have no need of you"; nor again the head to the feet, "I have no need of you." 22 No, much rather, those members of the body which seem to be weaker are necessary.

The Apostle Paul does not spare any pains in authoritatively declaring wholeness to the Church at Corinth. We are said to be one body with many members. As ministers and saints understand this concept, we will cease to compete for titles and simply recognize that all of us have a place within the community in which we must function. We must all understand how dependent we are upon one another because as we comprehend this we will rid our communities of competition and vengeance. If the covenant community is going to carry out the God-given vision that is attached to the house, the house must be willing to come together in unity.

Psalm 133:1,3
1 Behold, how good and how pleasant it is for brethren to dwell together in unity! . . . 3 For there the LORD commanded the blessing—Life forevermore.

Unity brings forth life, but not just any kind of life. The word for life used in verse three is *chay* which is strength and freshness. Interestingly enough, this word chay is also a noun that can be used in the singular feminine sense or in the plural masculine sense. Again, the covenant community though many is one body. We are not just any body, but we are the body of Christ, the corporate man.

This degree of unity that David is calling to our attention goes beyond just coming together for a situational event; rather this unity is to become a way of living. Until covenant community becomes a lifestyle, at best it is just another gathering of individuals that produces nothing more than fellowship coupled with disarray, disorder, and dysfunctionalism. On the contrary, when the covenant community takes on the lifestyle of unity, the community gives birth to something greater, or better said, someone greater than individual ideas can attain.

The covenant community begins as a vision given by God to the set ministry of the house. As mentioned in chapter two of this book, the set ministry is responsible for clearly communicating the vision of the house as it continues to evolve. The ability to respond correctly belongs to the people who must have faith in God. It is quite difficult to be a part of a true covenant community without having faith in the leader and the vision that is communicated while at the same time claiming to have faith in God who is the giver of the leader and the vision.

Habakkuk 2:2-4

2 Then the LORD answered me and said: "Write the vision and make it plain on tablets, that he may run who reads it. 3 For the vision is yet for an appointed time; but at the end it will speak, and it will not lie. Though it tarries, wait for it; because it will surely come; it will not tarry." 4 Behold the proud, His soul is not upright in him, but the just shall live by his faith.

As we corporately come together to fulfill the God-given vision, we manifest something or as I said earlier, someone greater than we could accomplish as individuals. Notice that what begins as a vision in Habakkuk becomes a manifestation in Hebrews.

Hebrews 10:37-39

37 "For yet a little while, And He who is coming will come and will not tarry. 38 Now the just shall live by faith; But if anyone draws back, My soul has no pleasure in him." 39 But we are not of those who draw back to perdition, but of those who believe to the saving of the soul.

As we look at Habakkuk and Hebrews, we notice that the wording of both texts is quite similar. One of the immediate differences of the two texts is the use of the words it and He. Habakkuk points to it—vision, while the writer of Hebrews points to He—Christ (the corporate man).

Hebrews 2:10-12, KJV

*10 For **it became him**, for whom are all things, and by whom are all things, in bringing many sons unto glory, to make the captain of their salvation perfect through sufferings. 11 For both he that sanctifieth and they who are sanctified are all of one: for which cause he is not ashamed to call them brethren, 12 Saying, I will declare thy name unto my brethren, in the midst of the church will I sing praise unto thee.*

In chapter seven, we went back to the tabernacle of Moses to foster our understanding of the one bread principle. As we looked at the tabernacle, we began to perceive that the covenant community, at least on the local church level (we will look at the global covenant community in a later chapter), is found in the inner court. It is noteworthy that the inner court is available to the priests who will see to the candlesticks, bread, and incense. However, if we are ever going to proceed beyond this realm, which must be our drive for perfecting this dimension, we must understand that we can not enter the most holy place as individual priests with our own agenda. Only the high priest could enter behind the veil, which is the dimension of the Kingdom.

As the covenant community begins to walk fully in the life giving power of true unity, we will manifest the true body of Christ in the earth. Thus, as long as we remain we, we can never come to the fullness of the Most Holy Place. This is why vision is so important. The vision of the house must come from God and we have to embrace the vision of the house if we are going to fulfill covenant community. Now, it overtakes us and becomes Him, which gives us access to the glorious third dimension of the tabernacle which is the dimension of Kingdom manifestation.

Ephesians 4:1-6,11-15, NKJV

1 I, therefore, the prisoner of the Lord, beseech you to walk worthy of the calling with which you were called, 2 with all lowliness and gentleness, with longsuffering, bearing with one another in love, 3 endeavoring to keep the unity of the Spirit in the bond of peace. 4 There is one body and one Spirit, just as you were called in one hope of your calling; 5 one Lord, one faith, one baptism; 6 one God and Father of all, who is above all, and through all, and in you all.

11 And He Himself gave some to be apostles, some prophets, some evangelists, and some pastors and teachers, 12 for the equipping of the saints for the work of ministry, for the edifying of the body of Christ, 13 till we all come to the unity of the faith and of the knowledge of the Son of God, to a perfect man, to the measure of the stature of the fullness of Christ; 14 that we should no longer be children, tossed to and fro and carried about with every wind of doctrine, by the trickery of men, in the cunning craftiness of deceitful plotting, 15 but, speaking the truth in love, may grow up in all things into Him who is the head—Christ

Don't miss the exhortation of the Apostle Paul. He begins chapter four with a strong plea for unity. As we reach the purpose for which Jesus gave gifts unto men, we discover that the objective of the ascension gifts is to bring "we" to the fullness of Christ, who is the head. No longer can we afford to have a huge chasm in our ministries that keep the saints infantile as ministers continue to deprive the saints of the necessary nutrients whereby growth is inevitable. If we are to come to a place of true unity and power so that we can manage the weight of headship, we must begin by equipping the saints to carry out their ministries. As we all posture ourselves to carryout our God given assignments in the earth, we may assume the position to function as a supplying joint of the body. Our love must abound more and more to the end that we become a source of supply one for another. Through the effectual edification supplied by every functioning joint, the body of Christ comes together to bring forth a glorious manifestation.

Matthew 8:20, NKJV

20 And Jesus said to him, "Foxes have holes and birds of the air have nests, but the Son of Man has nowhere to lay His head."

How long will the church allow this statement to be true? The Apostle Paul says in verse 13 of Ephesians 4 that we will perpetually remain immature, unable to carry His mature head, until we come to the unity of the faith. Our communities cannot afford to be a continuous playground for continual infantile behavior perpetuated by enthusiasm driven ministers who seek to keep the people entertained as opposed to seeing them grow up. Church of the living God, we can't afford to continue screaming as we enjoy getting dizzy on the same merry-go-round of meaninglessness. On the contrary we have a mission that must be fulfilled, to see to it that His government and peace increases to no end. Every joint must come to know his assignment in fulfilling this mandate. We have the mission of lifting Him up so that He may draw those that need to be drawn. This drawing points to the heavy gravitational pull of the corporate man in the Kingdom of God.

Numbers 7:89, NKJV

89 Now when Moses went into the tabernacle of meeting to speak with Him, he heard the voice of One speaking to him from above the mercy seat that was on the ark of the Testimony, from between the two cherubim; thus He spoke to him.

2 Kings 19:15, NKJV

15 Then Hezekiah prayed before the LORD, and said: "O LORD God of Israel, the One who dwells between the cherubim, You are God, You alone, of all the kingdoms of the earth. You have made heaven and earth.

The ark of God dwelt behind the veil in the Most Holy Place. This ark represented the government of God in the earth. Israel was guaranteed victory in battle provided they carried the ark of God with them and remained faithful to the order of God. God promised that he would dwell between the cherubim in the mercy seat as the Lord of hosts. Notice, there is only one throne in the Most Holy Place, it is reserved for God alone! There is only one priest who ministers before this throne, and that is the great High Priest. You say, the High Priest is Jesus and I say you are absolutely right. Therefore, if we are going behind this veil at all, we have to die to our selves on the altar of vision that we may enter into the bleeding side of Christ and grow up in Him. Our desire must be a longing for the glorious manifestation of God that will revolutionize the church and ultimately the world. The manifestation of the High Priest will be more and more evident as we, the royal priesthood, begin to step into destiny and come together as the remembered body of Christ.

Ex 28:33-35 NKJV

33 And upon its hem you shall make pomegranates of blue, purple, and scarlet, all around its hem, and bells of gold between them all around: 34 a golden bell and a pomegranate, a golden bell and a pomegranate, upon the hem of the robe all around. 35 And it shall be upon Aaron when he ministers, and its sound will be heard when he goes into the holy place before the LORD and when he comes out, that he may not die.

The garment of the High Priest gives us a clear picture of the necessary balance in the gifts and fruit of the spirit. One of the challenges in the church has to do with powerful demonstrations that are not backed by a life of spiritual produce. We have a great tendency in the church to be attracted to the gifts that an individual may walk in. It is imperative that we begin to note that there is a need for a balance in gifts and fruit. We should not focus primarily on the gifts of the spirit at the expense of the fruit of the spirit.

1 Corinthians 13:1 NKJV

Though I speak with the tongues of men and of angels, but have not love, I have become sounding brass or a clanging cymbal.

Behind the veil we find the essence of who God is. God is love. As we behold the glory of the Lord, we are transformed. His glory is seen in his love. Therefore, we too must begin to appropriate the love of Christ. We are to be a kingdom of kings and priests who demonstrate and celebrate the love of God.

CHAPTER 8

Assembly Required

Hebrews 10:24-25, NKJV
24 And let us consider one another in order to stir up love and good works, 25 not forsaking the assembling of ourselves together, as is the manner of some, but exhorting one another, and so much the more as you see the Day approaching.

For some, our savior gave his life on the cross so that we could have church and have it more frequently. Beloved, I do not believe that God was manifest in the flesh to live in a world of chaos just to suffer, die, and resurrect so that a few miserable people could gather on a Sunday morning to mourn their pitiful lives with hopes to one day go "ova yonda." Fundamentally, we should endeavor to be actively associated with Christian fellowship in terms of attending church gatherings whether in sanctuaries or living rooms. However, just going to church can not be the sum total of the life of a child of God. Is there a greater purpose for the life of Christ? Is it possible that He came to introduce the world to something greater than church services? This book is designed to take the idea of regular gatherings and fellowships to a greater dimension of fulfillment. This chapter, consequently, will take us beyond the local building in which we gather for worship and fellowship without belittling our regular gatherings. No doubt about it, the Lord draws His people together for fellowship, worship, and edification.

We must understand the greater purpose for our gathering that we may fulfill what the Lord has ordained. Let's expand our borders to an understanding that our worship is not just something we do until it is time to hear the preacher. When we adjust our mentality regarding worship, we will change our attitude towards the gathering of the covenant community thus adjusting how we fly off the deep end when some are not able to be in attendance due to other obligations. If we have to demand attendance to the point of condemning those absent to a life void of the possibility of ever moving into the greater things of God, perhaps we are having gatherings but not to true assemblies

Ephesians 4:16, NKJV

16 from whom the whole body, joined and knit together by what every joint supplies, according to the effective working by which every part does its share, causes growth of the body for the edifying of itself in love.

I will never forget the day I received a shocking revelation as the newly elected vice-president of the Student Government Association at Texas Wesleyan University. Oh how excited I was as the newly elected president decided that I too should have a desk in the executive office! The subsequent events proved to be less exciting yet very enlightening. As we shopped for a desk, we ultimately made a decision to purchase a small but elegant computer desk. Much to our surprise, the man went to the back of the store and brought back a white box that had a picture of my desk on it. Immediately I inquired as to what I was supposed to do with the box. He then pointed out to me that everything I needed was in the box. While that sounded good, all I had was a bunch of pieces. That is until I got the revelation from a label on the box that read, "assembly required." Oh how disappointed I was to learn that what I desired to see holistically was going to require more than just having all of the pieces, but would require assembling. Sounds like some of our Sunday morning and mid-week gatherings, doesn't it? We beg and plea for people to show up by promising them that we are going to have a good time. Or better yet, God is going to bless us. If these promises are not motivating enough, we then move to fear tactics. We threaten people that they have to show up or else face eternal damnation. Perhaps something is missing from the gathering which makes many not have an internal desire to show up. Could it be that while we have a gathering we are like my desk, just in a box!

The writer of Hebrews does not merely instruct us to gather; on the contrary we are instructed to assemble. Leadership must do a better job of relating the message of assembly to the people of God within our covenant communities. It is not just showing up because the pastor says to show up, rather it is the joining of a holy assembly before the Lord as we assemble unto Him. Each joint is to supply its necessary element which causes increase in the body. As long as the assembly is just the coming together to listen to the one man band and celebrate his giftedness in the presentation of the gospel, we will forever see many casualties along the way as people get bored and tired of the same old, same old.

What is the assembly that it is so important that we ought not to forsake it? The Greek word for assembly here is the word epi-sunagoge. The prefix epi is defined as a superimposition, as a relation of distribution, that which is above or over. The suffix sunagoge is a gathering, meeting, or assembly. Thus the epi-sunagogue is the superimposition of the above assembly upon the lower assembly. Our coming together should be more than just our coming together. Rather, when we gather the heavenly host gathers to superimpose itself upon us. This invasion of heaven on earth only happens when there is a true gathering of those of like precious faith who desire not just to gather but to come into the fullness of the glory of God.

Matthew 16:18-19
18 And I also say to you that you are Peter, and on this rock I will build My church, and the gates of Hades shall not prevail against it. 19 And I will give you the keys of the kingdom of heaven, and whatever you bind on earth will be bound in heaven, and whatever you loose on earth will be loosed in heaven."

This text has been used perhaps more than any to discuss the purpose of Christ's coming to the earth: to establish church. Perhaps we should look closer to discover that His purpose was not church, but rather the establishment of the real church which will release keys of the kingdom: his real purpose. As the covenant community gathers, there should be a release of keys that will cause a superimposing of the Kingdom on the church. As this happens, we begin to perceive the finished work of God in the heavenlies. Many misinterpret verse 19 to suggest that the church monopolizes heaven; thus, heaven has to respond according to what the church says. Rather with this superimposition comes a clear view of heaven which the church follows after. When the church lines up, divine agreement is manifested and heaven backs the church because the church has ceased to be merely an earthly existent fellowship.

One early morning while I was in prayer the Lord caused me to perceive that the keys were not keys to the Kingdom but keys of how the Kingdom operates. Therefore, what we really have the authority to bind and loose is the Kingdom! You say how is that possible? Simple, those who perceive the Kingdom to be afar off have bound it in heaven thus rendering the Kingdom inapplicable in their present reality. However, those of us who loose the Kingdom to manifest in our lives in the earth do not regulate the Kingdom to heaven.

Acts 2:1-5, NKJV
1When the Day of Pentecost had fully come, they were all with one accord in one place. 2 And suddenly there came a sound from heaven, as of a rushing mighty wind, and it filled the whole house where they were sitting. 3 Then there appeared to them divided

tongues, as of fire, and one sat upon each of them. 4 And they were all filled with the Holy Spirit and began to speak with other tongues, as the Spirit gave them utterance. 5 And there were dwelling in Jerusalem Jews, devout men, from every nation under heaven.

The day of Pentecost is a glorious illustration of the superimposition of heaven on the church, or rather the upper gathering on the lower gathering. The key of the Kingdom that unlocked heaven in this case, which is the driving agent of this entire book, is oneness. The superimposition of the heavenly assembly was so great that the expression of heaven took on verbal utterances that caused people from various nations to hear in their native language. Notice, that as you read further into Acts chapter 2 there was no need for a huge advertising budget. When there is a true assembly taking place beyond this natural realm, people will be drawn to the gravitational pull of the general assembly. We will explore this general assembly in greater detail in another chapter as well. For now, let's continue with the concept of oneness as a key that unlocks that heavenly superimposition.

2 Chronicles 5:1-6, 13-14, NKJV

1 Now Solomon assembled the elders of Israel and all the heads of the tribes, the chief fathers of the children of Israel, in Jerusalem, that they might bring the ark of the covenant of the LORD up from the City of David, which is Zion. 3 Therefore all the men of Israel assembled with the king at the feast, which was in the seventh month. 4 So all the elders of Israel came, and the Levites took up the ark. 5 Then they brought up the ark, the tabernacle of meeting, and all the holy furnishings that were in the tabernacle. The priests and the Levites brought them up. 6 Also King Solomon, and all the congregation of Israel who were assembled with him before the ark, were sacrificing sheep and oxen that could not be counted or numbered for multitude. 13 indeed it came to pass, when the trumpeters and singers were as one, to make one sound to be heard in praising and thanking the LORD, and when they lifted up their voice with the trumpets and cymbals and instruments of music, and praised the LORD, saying: "For He is good, For His mercy endures forever," that the house, the house of the LORD, was filled with a cloud, 14 so that the priests could not continue ministering because of the cloud; for the glory of the LORD filled the house of God.

Solomon has completed the building of the temple and has assembled the priests and Levites to bring the ark of God into the Most Holy Place. The scriptures are clear that again the key of oneness unlocks heaven and brings forth a glorious demonstration. This demonstration is in the form of a cloud. Clouds metaphorically speak of the glory of the Lord. Solomon is dedicating the temple with the assembly and suddenly there was a superimposition! So great was the cloud, that the normal procedures could not be carried out. When heaven superimposes itself, there goes the agenda of men!

Three heads of families are mentioned in particular in verse 12 that I would like to briefly examine. Asaph's name means Jehovah has gathered. Heman's name means faithfully building up. Jeduthun is the praising one. These three speak of the covenant community. Our communities should be houses that have been gathered by God for the purpose of establishment and edification as we unite in perpetual praise and divine worship.

I have personally been in gatherings where a true assembly took place. We all gathered with no agenda of man's wisdom. Perhaps this is the necessary key to a heavenly manifestation—our agendas must cease to be top priority. Perhaps we really should seek first the Kingdom. In one particular gathering, someone began to sing a song of praise unto the Lord with all sincerity. As she sang, those who were in attendance at the time began to join in with her praise. Suddenly, we were all aware that we were not in the room alone. As a matter of fact, several of us began to realize that we were not in the same room. The Lord began to speak to us through prophetic utterance in such a way that many had to lay prostrate before the Lord. One young man began break dancing in the middle of the floor! I cannot exhaust everything that transpired so I will conclude by saying when the higher assembly joins in with the lower assembly, those who make up the lower assembly will be transformed and elevated. If the covenant community can get to the place where praise and worship is left in its pure state of being God centered, then the Lion of the tribe of Judah can manifest Himself in a great and glorious way through a superimposition. When this happens effectively, we will cease gathering just to have church but through a superimposition of heaven carry out the agenda of the Kingdom of God and further see the power thereof. We must take a further look at glory as it is exhibited in clouds throughout scripture to understand this superimposition or this "super position" God wants to put us in.

Exodus 40:17-21, 26-34

17 And it came to pass in the first month of the second year, on the first day of the month, that the tabernacle was raised up. 18 So Moses raised up the tabernacle, fastened its sockets, set up its boards, put in its bars, and raised up its pillars. 19 And he spread out the tent over the tabernacle and put the covering of the tent on top of it, as the LORD had commanded Moses. 20 He took the Testimony and put it into the ark, inserted the poles through the rings of the ark, and put the mercy seat on top of the ark. 21 And he brought the ark into the tabernacle, hung up the veil of the covering, and partitioned off the ark of the Testimony, as the LORD had commanded Moses.

26 He put the gold altar in the tabernacle of meeting in front of the veil; 27 and he burned sweet incense on it, as the LORD had commanded Moses. 28 He hung up the screen at the door of the tabernacle. 29 And he put the altar of burnt offering before the door of the tabernacle of the tent of meeting, and offered upon it the burnt offering and the grain offering, as the LORD had commanded Moses. 30 He set the laver between the tabernacle of meeting and the altar, and put water there for washing; 31 and Moses, Aaron, and his sons would wash their hands and their feet with water from it. 32 Whenever they went into the tabernacle of meeting, and when they came near the altar, they washed, as the LORD had commanded Moses. 33 And he raised up the court all around the tabernacle and the altar, and hung up the screen of the court gate. So Moses finished the work. 34 Then the cloud covered the tabernacle of meeting, and the glory of the LORD filled the tabernacle.

1 Thessalonians 4:15-18

15 For this we say to you by the word of the Lord, that we who are alive and remain until the coming of the Lord will by no means precede those who are asleep. 16 For the Lord Himself will descend from heaven with a shout, with the voice of an archangel, and with the trumpet of God. And the dead in Christ will rise first. 17 Then we who are alive and remain shall be caught up together with them in the clouds to meet the Lord in the air. And thus we shall always be with the Lord.

The objective here is not to debate eschatological concepts. I merely want us to seize a revelation beyond the end of the world as we have come to know it to foster our understanding of this powerful truth. Is it possible that the only way for us to fully appreciate 1 Thessalonians, we must tie it to Hebrews 12?

Hebrews 12:1

1 Therefore we also, since we are surrounded by so great a cloud of witnesses, let us lay aside every weight, and the sin which so easily ensnares us, and let us run with endurance the race that is set before us.

Is it possible that the coming of the Lord in 1 Thessalonians is not simply literal but possibly even spiritual? Is it possible that 1 Thessalonians further affirms the fact that we are to experience a heavenly superimposition as we gather corporately? Now don't leave me here because the traditional thinking mindset will not be open to the possibility of truth beyond that which we have embraced and accepted. If we look at this text coupled with Hebrews 12 we will emerge into a comprehension that promises to introduce a more fulfilling and glorious assembly of the redeemed of the Lord beyond what we have experienced heretofore. Hebrews 12 is clear that we are presently surrounded with a cloud of witnesses, not will be someday. Wait! Did you say a cloud of witnesses? Yes a cloud. These witnesses are the same as the asleep ones of 1 Thessalonians, perhaps the dead in Christ. Those of us who are alive are to be caught up together with them in the clouds. How did we go from cloud to clouds?

—

To understand this phenomenon we have to go back to the tabernacle of Moses again. Within the Inner Court, as mentioned briefly in chapter 3, we find the altar of incense. As the altar of incense burns, the smoke creates a cloud in the court. Seeing as how 1 Thessalonians was written by a Jew, no doubt he understood the symbolism of the cloud in respect to the tabernacle. The altar of incense speaks of our worship and intercession according to Revelation 5 and Psalm 141. Therefore, as we gather together as a covenant community in worship and intercession we create a cloud. It is crucial that we remain open to a fresh understanding of 1 Thessalonians. Our cloud of worship and intercession comes together with the cloud of witnesses and the Lord meets us in the air of worship! Let's look at a few more verses of scripture to see if we can validate this argument.

Luke 21:25-28

25 "And there will be signs in the sun, in the moon, and in the stars; and on the earth distress of nations, with perplexity, the sea and the waves roaring; 26 men's hearts failing them from fear and the expectation of those things which are coming on the earth, for the powers of the heavens will be shaken. 27 Then they will see the Son of Man coming in a cloud with power and great glory. 28 Now when these things begin to happen, look up and lift up your heads, because your redemption draws near."

Again, don't take off to eschatology on me right here. It is quite obvious that we live in the days of perplexities, failures of hearts, and roaring in the seas. What's the answer to this dilemma? A church that's afraid of what is going on in the world or a church that is just ready to get the heck out of here so that we don't have to deal with the insanity of our society. Neither of these can be the answer. We need to see a superimposition of heaven on earth. This superimposition is one of great power and glory.

How does this manifestation take place? Through the Son of Man coming in, not on, a cloud! As the church gathers unto the general assembly we will have a manifestation of the Son of Man among us through a heavenly superimposition. When this superimposition is released the community ceases to be made up of the sons of men but becomes the manifestation of the sons of God! This is clearly seen through the lifting up of our heads and the drawing near of our redemption. Redemption is not to take us away but rather to bring us into full liberation, deliverance, ransom—thus the manifestation of the sons of God. When the covenant community operates on this level, we will experience a glorious new church living in a glorious new day!

Before we leave this chapter, we should go back to 1 Thessalonians 4:16 now that we are examining that text without eschatological shades. "*. . . For the Lord Himself will descend from heaven with a shout, with the voice of an archangel,* *and with the trumpet of God . . ."* As you come to understand metaphors, types, and shadows throughout the scriptures, you will see that the trumpet is often indicative of the prophetic proclamation. Thus, the Lord descends from a heavenly dimension into the earth realm as the covenant community comes together as the voice of many waters with unity and harmony in praise and purpose. Let's come into order and begin to worship until our local gatherings are taken over by a heavenly superimposition. When we begin to experience the superimposition, we will see the "super position" that the church will function in. We will begin to manifest and walk as a greater authority in the earth as His government is increased. Perhaps, right now you are in a posture to read the book of revelation again.

Revelation 1:5-7, NKJV
5 To Him who loved us and washed us from our sins in His own blood, 6 and has made us kings and priests to His God and Father, to Him be glory and dominion forever and ever. 7 Behold, He is coming with clouds, and every eye will see Him, even they who pierced Him. And all the tribes of the earth will mourn because of Him. Even so, Amen.

CHAPTER 9

From Rocks to a Mountain

Throughout this book we have focused our attention on the local covenant community. I believe that we would do a great injustice not to unravel a greater truth and come to a higher place of understanding. While we must develop our local houses, we cannot become focused on the local at the expense of the complete denial of the greater, global covenant community, otherwise known as the Kingdom of God.

When we speak of vision with pastors, for the most part the vision is the same; reach the world with the gospel. While this is a very noble statement and definitely has its roots within the great commission given by our Lord, I think that there are some details or specifics that we may need to incorporate within the confines of our dialogue. Is it really possible for one local covenant community to reach the whole world? The obvious answer to this simple yet perplexing question is unfortunately, NO. The question is simple in its nature and yet it is quite perplexing due to the many covenant communities who feel that they, in isolation, will be able to reach the world. As I understand it, the earth's population is nearing 8 billion people. Clearly this phenomenal accomplishment of winning the world will require something far greater than a local covenant community. The reality is that every local community has its limitations. Consequently, we must seek another method to accomplish what Jesus left before us concerning winning the world.

I will not soon forget the message that brought life to me at a time of discontentment in terms of my then present state in ministry. I sensed an urgent need to attend "Rhema", a yearly conference in Dallas hosted by Bishop David E. Martin. The prophetic word of the Lord that came forth from the lips of Bishop Eddie L. Long, spoke so deep in the corridors of my soul that life began pumping inside of me, the likes of which I had never experienced previously.

While much brought life to me, I keenly remember his bold and challenging command in the spirit as he merged Deuteronomy 8:18 and Deuteronomy 15:6. It was just a point in the message, but it still resounds in my spirit. For the first time, I began to see that God had ordained the true church of God to rise up and subdue nations. No longer was my mindset stuck on just getting people saved to go to heaven someday, which he challenged as well, but a revolution had begun inside of me to see that what has been lost in the earth is the Kingdom which Jesus came to restore.

"You cannot lend to nations out of your personal account, which means God intends for the church to have a bank!" declared Bishop Long. Those words were overwhelmingly beyond anything that I had heard affirmed prior to that night. As we begin to conquer nations, we must perceive we cannot do this exclusively through our local churches. A nation must rise that is far superior to any nation that presently exists. Sounds like a job for the Kingdom of God, which manifests the will of God from the heavenly realm to the earthly!

Genesis 11:1, 5-9 NKJV
1 Now the whole earth had one language and one speech.

5 But the LORD came down to see the city and the tower which the sons of men had built. 6 And the LORD said, "Indeed the people are one and they all have one language, and this is what they begin to do; now nothing that they propose to do will be withheld from them. 7 Come, let Us go down and there confuse their language, that they may not understand one another's speech." 8 So the LORD scattered them abroad from there over the face of all the earth, and they ceased building the city. 9 Therefore its name is called Babel, because there the LORD confused the language of all the earth; and from there the LORD scattered them abroad over the face of all the earth.

The power of oneness is that virtually anything becomes possible. While the building of this tower was certainly not in line with the will of God, the reality is that because of their powerful display of oneness they were actually accomplishing what they set out to do. There goal was to build this tower so as to challenge God and to build a name for themselves. Our objective in this hour is not an attempt to establish our own system of government in defiance against God; rather it is to unite for the purpose of synergistically appropriating the government of God within the earth. This, when done with the overwhelming force of oneness, according to verse 6 can be done without any possible defense to stop us.

Luke 11:17, NKJV
17 But He, knowing their thoughts, said to them: "Every kingdom divided against itself is brought to desolation, and a house divided against a house falls.

The denial of the successful completion in building this tower was the result of confusion and division. As God commends the oneness, he must put a stop to the agenda because it was out of order. As we look through the scriptures as well as throughout history, we notice that defeat is always the bi-product of division. In Second Chronicles twenty there is the story of Jehosophat coming under the attack of three armies who have united together to defeat the people of God. Immediately, Jehosophat brought the people of God before the Lord in a spirit of unity. As the oneness of the people of God began moving towards the battlefield, confusion was released upon the children of Moab, Ammon, and Mount Seir. The result, oneness prevails!

Imagine what we could do as the people of God if we would come to the place where we have true unity amongst the saints without regard for glorified fraternities and sororities, otherwise known as denominations and other religious banners. Some are of the opinion that this can never happen with men. First, let us remember as the people of faith that with men things are not possible but with God all things become possible. Also, we must remember the heart of Jesus as he prays to the Father concerning the saints.

John 17:20-23, NKJV

20 "I do not pray for these alone, but also for those who will believe in Me through their word; 21 that they all may be one, as You, Father, are in Me, and I in You; that they also may be one in Us, that the world may believe that You sent Me. 22 And the glory which You gave Me I have given them, that they may be one just as We are one: 23 I in them, and You in Me; that they may be made perfect in one, and that the world may know that You have sent Me, and have loved them as You have loved Me."

The responsibility of presenting a glorious appearance of Christ to the world is a very major and challenging one. This prayer, as is the purpose of this book, should provoke us to come to a greater place of oneness, the likes of which the world has never seen before. While looking at the Tower of Babel model, the problem that you may see is that God confused the language which creates a major hindrance in coming to the place of powerful unity that will truly glorify and perpetuate the government of God. My brothers and sisters this is exactly why the day of Pentecost came to manifest.

Acts 2:1-6, KJV

2:1 And when the day of Pentecost was fully come, they were all with one accord in one place. 2 And suddenly there came a sound from heaven as of a rushing mighty wind, and it filled all the house where they were sitting. 3 And there appeared unto them cloven tongues like as of fire, and it sat upon each of them. 4 And they were all filled with the Holy Ghost, and began to speak with other tongues, as the Spirit gave them utterance.

5 And there were dwelling at Jerusalem Jews, devout men, out of every nation under heaven. 6 Now when this was noised abroad, the multitude came together, and were confounded, because that every man heard them speak in his own language.

Just as God confused the language, He is able to put the languages back together again according as He purposes. The sovereign God demonstrates that his desire is for oneness that is subject to His power. So mighty is the sealing force of the spirit that many standing around began to hear those speaking with other tongues in their native languages. God understands that if oneness of language was the key for the tower, it will take a restoration of the languages to get another city built. This is why so many historically exclusive denominations are beginning to see that there are other organizations that have been raised by the Father to do great things for the Kingdom as well. Now, it is quite difficult to distinguish one sect of church from another because many are beginning to see in the spirit and speak the same language.

Matthew 16:18
18 And I say also unto thee, That thou art Peter, and upon this rock I will build my church; and the gates of hell shall not prevail against it.

The irony between the title of this chapter and Matthew 16:18 is that Jesus here refers to one universal church whereas the chapter title speaks indicatively of the present reality of the church as we know it. As opposed to their being one universal church, we have fractioned or rather de-nomid (divided through numbering) the holy nation of 1 Peter 2:9. I believe however that this writing, along with many greater writings and prophetic messages that are being released, is pointing to the greater call of God, which is a holy nation. Many have built their churches around their doctrine, constitution, style, format, etc. at the expense of becoming exclusive without regard for the global covenant community, the overall Kingdom of God.

We have come to a glorious time in the Kingdom where God is gathering men and women from all over the globe of like precious faith and giving them an amalgamated heart of flesh as opposed to the segmented heart of stone. We are moving now, beyond individual rocks which see very little success in the true scope of fulfilling the great commission, to the forming of a glorious, majestic mountain.

Jeremiah 50:5, KJV
5 They shall ask the way to Zion with their faces thitherward, saying, Come, and let us join ourselves to the LORD in a perpetual covenant that shall not be forgotten.

Those who are hearing the trumpet of God for this hour are becoming as those of Jeremiah 50. We must get the city built, but it is going to take repentance from dead works unto the Kingdom of God. This will only happen as we join ourselves in the Lord, not under some segmented banner, but the Lord himself must be our banner. As we join in this perpetual covenant, we must understand the sacrifice. We must perceive that where the body of Christ has been thus far is less than the fullness of what God has ordained. There will be those who will hear, those who will not hear immediately, and perhaps few who will not hear at all. Those who are hearing the voice of God speaking as a trumpet must be willing to sacrifice their religious reputation for the common good of the global community. This type of perpetual covenant is a force to be reckoned with because it cannot and will not be stopped. Never has the world seen a hurricane, earthquake, or war that can do the type of damage that true covenant amongst the saints will do to the powers of darkness. Fervently, we must conduct ourselves in a manner that will exhibit true eternal covenant that is void of ulterior motive and denominational distinction. To accomplish this, we must have a longing to achieve a higher calling than someday dying and going to heaven. Perhaps the desire of those involved in building the tower of Babel should more purely become our desire with proper motive and purpose. The goal: build a city or better yet, become one, not to get up and go to a city but to become a city whose builder, maker, and sustainer is God himself.

Matthew 5:14, NKJV
14 "You are the light of the world. A city that is set on a hill cannot be hidden.

Psalm 125:1, KJV
1 They that trust in the LORD shall be as mount Zion, which cannot be removed, but abideth for ever.

Jesus clarifies for us that we are not called to be mediocre or irrelevant; rather we are called to manifest excellence and influence. As this is understood, we will seek the more of Christ that he may release his glorious rule and reign within the earth. For many, Zion is nothing more than something that we get to enjoy looking at with hopes of someday going there when it's all over.

Perhaps we should be careful to note that Jesus here in Matthew does not promise we are going to a city someday. He clearly states that we are a city. What city are we to be? We are to be the City of David, which is Zion according to 2 Chronicles 5:2. This city is like no other. It is a beautiful stronghold that is a joy to the whole earth. While it may sound as if I am calling for the complete annihilation of denominations, I'm more concerned about the nation coming together. How will this happen? It is going to start when the city church is formed of the churches within the many regions of the world. This mountain is not going to be formed until we first manifest the city church on a hill. The city church will be formed as heads of local covenant communities come together in purpose to manifest momentum in bringing forth regional transformation. God has placed generals in each city that must be recognized and brought together.

Psalm 50:2 NKJV
2 Out of Zion, the perfection of beauty, God will shine forth.

Psalm 48:2, NKJV
2 Beautiful in elevation, the joy of the whole earth is Mount Zion on the sides of the north, The city of the great King.

The city church is crucial but not the end of all things. Just as the rocks come together to create a hill, so also hills come together to create a mountain. As we manifest this glorious mountain in the earth, God is able to shine forth with majesty and splendor. All of creation is waiting for this triumphant day when we manifest sonship in the earth as a royal priesthood and a holy nation. When this happens, we as kings in the earth will bow and cast down our crowns to the King of kings. This place requires much humility, yet it is a beautiful elevation. As we decrease, the plans of the Father increase.

Ecclesiastes 3:11a, NKJV
11 He has made everything beautiful in its time.

It is time to manifest the glorious Kingdom of God in a new and powerful way. The old order has expired and the new order is here. We must choose to put down our convenient methodology of doing church as usual and adhere to the trumpet that is blowing in Zion. The declaration of the Lord for this hour is clear—come unto Zion! Until one is willing to forsake all and follow him, one will forever wander in the wilderness of religious activity and never come into the land that God has ordained.

Hebrews 12:18,22-24, KJV
18 For ye are not come unto the mount that might be touched, and that burned with fire, nor unto blackness, and darkness, and tempest, 22 But ye are come unto mount [Z]ion, and unto the city of the living God, the heavenly Jerusalem, and to an innumerable company of angels, 23 To the general assembly and church of the firstborn, which are written in heaven, and to God the Judge of all, and to the spirits of just men made perfect, 24 And to Jesus the mediator of the new covenant, and to the blood of sprinkling, that speaketh better things than that of Abel.

Coming unto Zion is not traveling like tourists to see Mount Everest. We are not just beholding a mountain but we are becoming the mountain of God. We are becoming the city of God where he inhabits and rules as the governor of the nation. The contrast of Sinai and Zion is illustrated by the writer of Hebrews as a glorious demonstration of the old covenant and the new covenant. God has not summoned us to a place of darkness; rather He has commissioned us to come to a place where we become the light that we behold. Not only are we becoming, but the closer we get to manifestation, the larger we become. People will stand in awe and amazement as they see this mountain grow and glow as sons and daughters continue to come forth.

Isaiah 66:8, KJV

8 Who hath heard such a thing? Who hath seen such things? Shall the earth be made to bring forth in one day? Or shall a nation be born at once? For as soon as Zion travailed, she brought forth her children.

As we manifest Zion in the earth, we will accomplish the great prophetic word of the Lord concerning Christ in Isaiah 9:7—Of the increase of His government and peace, there will be no end . . .

CHAPTER 10

Glory Revealed

John 17:22-23
22 And the glory which You gave Me I have given them, that they may be one just as We are one: 23 I in them, and You in Me; that they may be made perfect in one, and that the world may know that You have sent Me, and have loved them as You have loved Me.

The Introduction of this book references the Garden of Eden, which was the place of the initializing of covenant community. By the time we get to John 17, everything has gone full circle. The community was damaged in a garden and is repaired in a garden. Jesus said, "I am come for that which was lost." What was lost? Before answering, please notice that Jesus does not say I am come for them rather he said for that. What was lost was identity within the Kingdom of God. Therefore, Jesus came with a two fold purpose, to restore the Kingdom and man's identity within that Kingdom. Those who are "lost" wanderers will return to God's Kingdom as soon as they behold something amazing.

John 1:14
14 And the Word became flesh and dwelt among us, and we beheld His glory, the glory as of the only begotten of the Father, full of grace and truth.

According to John 1:14, glory is observable. Therefore, we conclude that glory is the visible expression of an invisible essence. Jesus, the son of God is the physical expression of God who is spirit. The reason Jesus is called the son and God is called the Father is because spirit is of a higher order than that which is natural. Spirit gave birth and produced natural; therefore, the natural is the offspring of spirit. The power of this reality lies within the understanding that Jesus came through Mary but he did not come from Mary. Jesus housed within his body the seed of God!

The seed was so powerful that even as an infant his arrival stirred up Herod and his kingdom. Wise men and shepherds will respond to the news of the seed of God in Bethlehem. He's less than two years old but fear and torment have already gripped the hearts of those who knew that their time was now limited, while at the same time exciting many to know that their deliverance was nigh. So much activity begins to take place it the region because of the introduction of Immanuel, God with us.

At age 12, the seed has sprouted into a young man who is strong in spirit and full of wisdom and grace. We find the beginning stages of his influence released as he sits among the scholars in Jerusalem who are astonished at the level of understanding that comes from this young man. Now, for the first time, those of us who were not present during his lifetime get an opportunity to be a part of the words that come from the lips of Jesus. He affirms that he understands who he is by declaring that he must be about his Father's business. Ironically, he will mature naturally as the son of a carpenter while at the same time maturing in the spirit as the son of God.

This maturation process brings Immanuel to the Jordan River at age 30 where he will be baptized by John the Baptist. As Jesus comes up from the water, the heavens open and God declares, "You are my beloved Son." The book of Hebrews says he is the "express image" of God. From this point many signs and wonders will accompany the life of Jesus, the Son of God. The Message translation records John 1:14 and 18 as, "We saw the glory with our own eyes, the one-of-a-kind glory, like Father, like Son . . . This one-of-a-kind God-Expression, who exists at the very heart of the Father, has made him plain as day."

I used to hear people use the phrase, one of a kind, to refer to the uniqueness of an individual or object. Most times this phrase was used to point to a quality of uniqueness or extraordinary value. I have now come to understand that one of kind does not mean only but rather **one** of a **kind**. The word kind is a root for our word, kindred. Jesus is uniquely and extraordinarily the expression or personification of God; however, he is not to walk in this glory alone. He is the preeminent one of a kind of species.

Hebrews 2:10-11

10 For it was fitting for Him, for whom are all things and by whom are all things, in bringing many sons to glory, to make the captain of their salvation perfect through sufferings. 11 For both He who sanctifies and those who are being sanctified are all of one, for which reason He is not ashamed to call them brethren

The Apostle Paul says the same thing:

Romans 8:29
29 For whom He foreknew, He also predestined to be conformed to the image of His Son, that He might be the firstborn among many brethren.

Without a doubt, Jesus came to restore the sonship identity of fallen man in the community or Kingdom of God. For many, this simply means that Jesus came to save us and give us our ticket to heaven. The greater reality is that Jesus came to show us that a new species of man is emerging. This kind of man recognizes a reality much more superior than last name association. This kind perceives that Jesus did not come to be simply celebrated, but he came to be duplicated. He said to his disciples as they celebrated him in John 20, "As the Father has sent Me, so send I you". The Father sent his Son as his duplication, as his expression. We are called and sent by God in "like Father, like son" glory.

Isaiah 6:3
3 And one cried to another and said: "Holy, holy, holy is the Lord of hosts; The whole earth is full of His glory!"

Ladies and gentlemen, the prophetic declaration of heaven concerning the earth is that the glory is here. Why do we not see it now? The glory is here in seed form. The world is waiting for a manifestation! The world is echoing in many ways, "the seed is good, but the fruit is better." Only when we acknowledge our kinship or oneness with Christ will we access the glory thereof. The Hebrew writer acknowledges the communal truth that he who sanctifies and the millions, yea even billions, who are being sanctified, are all of one. The people of God are called to develop in truth and once again manifest as Jesus did, the brilliant, dazzling, extraordinary, essence of God.

Romans 8:18-19
18 For I consider that the sufferings of this present time are not worthy to be compared with the glory which shall be revealed in us. 19 For the earnest expectation of the creation eagerly waits for the revealing of the sons of God.

The world is not waiting on more church buildings, more PA systems on street corners, and certainly not more people handing out booklets that promote a fire insurance policy in case of rapture. All of creation is waiting on a people to rise from obscurity to prominence. There must come an unveiling of God not only with us but in and through us. Jesus said that we are, as he is, the light of the world. Everything that the son of God was we are to be!

Hebrews 1:3
3 who being the brightness of His glory and the express image of His person, and upholding all things by the word of His power, when He had by Himself purged our sins, sat down at the right hand of the Majesty on high,

He saved us that we may represent Him to the world. We are to carry His influence into every venue of the world. This puts the body of Christ in a much more offensive posture than one that struggles to simply maintain in the days of misfortune and adversity. My prayer is that as you have read through this book that faith has stirred inside of you to acknowledge that God is desirous of having expression through you. We are to be saved, sanctified, and shining like never before!

Matt 5:16
16 Let your light so shine before men, that they may see your good works and glorify your Father in heaven.

The glory of God revealed through us will provoke the world to glorifying God. We have the complete responsibility to point the world to God. This is not done through a series of religious services nor religious television programming. This responsibility is only carried out as we all press into the oneness that we have with the Father and manifest his glory though our lives. Jesus prays in John 17 and declares that when this unveiling takes place, the world will acknowledge the Father.

Perhaps in concern Romans 3:23 comes to mind, "All have sinned and fall short of the glory of God." That is definitely what the word of God says, but this simply further illustrates the point. Outside of our source it is impossible to function as the God-expression. Thus the Apostle Paul gives us very encouraging news in Colossians 1:27 as he causes us to understand that although in and of ourselves we fall short of glory, Christ in us is the hope of glory. Christ in us is the seed of glory, but it is not the glory. Remember, glory is observable. Christ revealed through us is the glory. We must learn to live and function from the inside out.

The dominant passion of the heart of Christ in the garden as he is in prayer is that we will walk in our identity within the Kingdom as being one with God. Religious thinking will make you feel that oneness with man is good but oneness with God is somehow heretical. One would be hard pressed to make that statement in lieu of the word of God.

Philippians 2:5-6

Let this mind be in you, which was also in Christ Jesus: 6 Who, being in the form of God, thought it not robbery to be equal with God:

We must do away with religious rhetoric that positions us to struggle and strain to simply live our lives with no other expectancy beyond dying and going to heaven. This type of thinking will not empower us to change our world as ambassadors of the Kingdom of God. We must begin hungering and thirsting for manifestation. We must approach everyday and every moment with a clear understanding that as He is, so are we. We are made in His image and after His likeness. We are the formation, expression, representation of God.

Psalm 82:6

I said, "You are gods, And all of you are children of the Most High."

This particular psalm opens up with a powerful proclamation.

Psalm 82:1

God stands in the congregation of the mighty; He judges among the gods.
Young's Literal Translation
God hath stood in the company of God, In the midst God doth judge.
English Standard Version
God has taken his place in the divine council
Darby
God standeth in the assembly of God, he judgeth among the gods.
Bible in Basic English
God is in the meeting-place of God; he is judging among the gods.

The sons of God are the company of God, the assembly of God, the divine council of God, the house of God, the community of God, the formation of God. God reproduces himself in a people who stand strong and mighty, ready to accomplish His purposes. Jesus understood this reality and prays earnestly for a people to come into the same oneness with God that he has. He even makes this profound statement, "I am the vine, and you are the branches." The branch is not made up of anything different than the vine. Branches are nothing more than the fruit bearing extensions of the source from which they come. These branches, so long as they remain attached in oneness to the vine will continually produce.

Galatians 5:22-23
22 But the fruit of the Spirit is love, joy, peace, longsuffering, kindness, goodness, faithfulness, 23 gentleness, self-control.

Fruit is produced by placing a seed in dirt. At first glance, this statement may appear a bit nebulous. Yet nothing can be said more poignant when you understand that God put the seed of himself within man. The Apostle Paul says this seed of the divine nature is a treasure in earthly vessels. Many of us are so sin conscious of our dirt that we cease to be God conscious of our spiritual reality. This is the result of low-level thinking that is only magnified by elementary preaching. When revelatory truth is released, the hearer must bring his thinking up. Therefore revelation detaches the soul from flesh focus to spirit focus!

Matthew 6:22 KJV
22 The light of the body is the eye: if therefore thine eye be single, thy whole body shall be full of light.

What are you focused on? If you're focused on you and God, you will only manifest partial light because you will always perceive your deficiencies and inadequacies. Jesus says proper perception will lead to proper illumination. Fullness is defined as being without lack or separation. If you're Adam in a garden, you will see no separation between you and God until you perceive your nakedness. If you're Peter you will walk on the water like Jesus until you perceive the doubt being released from the guys on the boat. This is why worship is critical for the people of God. Worship keeps us focused on the greatness of God.

2 Corinthians 3:18
18 But we all, with unveiled face, beholding as in a mirror the glory of the Lord, are being transformed into the same image from glory to glory, just as by the Spirit of the Lord.

We are called to give glory to God which will ultimately cause us to walk in the glory of God. Glory to God involves the release of our praise and worship with gratitude for all He has done and for who He is in our lives. However, this is not the glory of God. Glory to God is a means to move in the glory of God. The more we release of our spirit in worship, the more we increase our capacity to walk in the glory of God. No matter where you are in your pursuit of the Kingdom of God, know that beyond a doubt, you were made in the image of God. You must begin pulling down all imaginations! When you know whose image you walk in, everything less than glory is simply an imagination.

—

1 John 3:2 KJV

2 Beloved, now are we the sons of God, and it doth not yet appear what we shall be: but we know that, when he shall appear, we shall be like him; for we shall see him as he is.

Please don't put this off until the end of the world. Someone somewhere has to step into this glorious manifestation. I am not saying that there will not be an ultimate consummation of this scripture, but I am completely advocating that the process begins as soon as you put your eyes on Christ. The author of Hebrews says that we are to continue looking unto Jesus, the author and finisher of our faith. The seed must become a manifestation.

Revelation 21:10-11

10 And he carried me away in the Spirit to a great and high mountain, and showed me the great city, the holy Jerusalem, descending out of heaven from God, 11 having the glory of God. Her light was like a most precious stone, like a jasper stone, clear as crystal.

For many, John saw a city. For many, John saw a people. Let our hearts be consumed with the passion of Christ. We are the city; now let's go after the glory. Father, make us one.